Anger Anonymous
The Big Book on Anger Addiction

Dennis Ortman

For information, contact:

MSI Press
1760-F Airline Highway, 203
Hollister, CA 95023
Orders@MSIPress.com
Telephone/Fax: 831-886-2486

Library of Congress Control Number 2017943902

ISBN 9781950328093

cover design by Carl Leaver
cover photos: Shutterstock.com

Contents

INTRODUCTION

Anger Anonymous:
The Big Book on Anger Addiction

"Anyone can become angry—that is easy, but to be angry with the right person, and to the right degree, and at the right time, and for the right purpose, and in the right way— that is not within everybody's power and is not easy."

—Aristotle

Anger arises within us with a warning label: "Handle with extreme caution!" It is a fire that can give light and warmth to sustain life when well managed, or it can burn and incinerate when out of control. Anger possesses a power that fascinates and disturbs. Even though we witness its devastating effects in broken relationships, violence, and war, we relish the momentary sense of power we feel when enraged. "Anger is one letter short of danger," the saying goes.

Society respects anger's dangerous potential. It makes laws against violent behavior. Parents teach their children to manage their temper. Religion cautions against becoming slaves of passion and offers practices for developing self-control. Yet despite these warnings and our best efforts working with this difficult emotion, we may feel powerless in its grip. After suffering the devastating effects of its excess, we may secretly admit to ourselves, "I'm powerless over my anger, and my life has become unmanageable because of it." It may dawn on us that we are addicted to it.

A Personal Note

My own struggles with anger made writing this book a difficult personal journey. Reflecting on the meaning of anger and how to work with it effectively led me to a personal exploration. My anger frightened me, so I swallowed it. I did not recognize the depth of my fear and buried anger and their impact on my life. Without realizing it, my emotional life had become unmanageable.

Growing up, I received many confusing messages about anger. My father was a gentle, honest man—until he drank. Then he became a roaring and scary monster. Dr. Jekyll by day, he transformed to Mr. Hyde some nights. I later realized how much rage my father must have forced down behind his normally placid façade. He spent three years fighting the Germans during the war and undoubtedly suffered from post-traumatic stress disorder. He drank to drown his demons. My mother must have shared in his personal hell as she endured his drunken rages. She displayed her anger with criticisms and corrections. "If you do something, do it right," she used to say. That meant doing it her way.

I coped with the insecurity of my childhood by becoming a quiet, compliant, over-achieving child, "a good little boy." Terrified of becoming like my out of control father, I buried my anger so deep it escaped my notice. However, it leaked out in subtle ways. I enjoyed war movies, played with guns, and built a fort behind our garage. Thoughts of fighting and victory filled my young mind. In school, I would not tolerate anything less than an A grade. Playing sports and board games, I hated to lose. I secretly wanted to be the best at whatever I did and beat others. In short, I became a passive-aggressive perfectionist, often impatient with my own and others' foibles. The debris of judgmental thoughts floated around in my head.

As an adult I pursued noble helping professions, first as a priest, and then as a psychologist. I could preserve my "nice guy" image within my admired role. As I am becoming more aware and accepting of the gift of my own anger, I am anxious to share what I am learning. "We teach what we need to learn," wisdom tells us.

Jason's Story

Jason had worked at his computer sales company for ten years. He gained a reputation for being a hardworking, conscientious, and loyal employee. His sales figures were always near the top. When a sales manager position became available, Jason immediately applied for it, certain he would be promoted. His boss encouraged him to apply and seemed to suggest that the job was his for the taking.

When someone else was chosen for the job, Jason was stunned. What added insult to injury was the fact that the man chosen had worked at the company for only five years, and Jason had trained him. "That's unfair," Jason told himself and anyone who would listen. He felt betrayed by his boss and protested, "How could I have been passed over? You told me the job was mine!"

His boss could only offer lame apologies, "The higher ups have their own agenda."

After the initial disbelief and disappointment, anger set in. His wife and friends tried to comfort him, agreeing that it was unfair. Jason considered for a moment whether he should quit, but he was not confident he could find a comparable salary elsewhere. So he continued to go to work, but his heart was not in it as it was before. He could not shake the idea that he was treated unfairly. His resentment grew.

His preoccupation with the injustice invaded his sleep. He had dreams of throttling his boss. Each morning, he awakened tired and dreading the day. In the shower, he obsessed,

"How could this happen to me after all I gave to the company?" He became more irritable with his family. Everything seemed to annoy him. At work, he avoided his boss and the man who stole his job. He withdrew from his coworkers and spent as little time as possible at the office. Jason could not relax. He developed back and stomach pain. He sensed the anger was eating him alive.

Jason thought about his father, who had an explosive temper. He always told himself, "I'll never be like him." He learned to swallow his anger and always keep himself under control. He nurtured a calm façade that served him well in his profession. But with the loss of the promotion he had set his heart on, his tranquility evaporated.

Now the resentment took over his life, and he felt powerless to let it go.

Anger as a Drug

Many label anger a negative emotion because it can be as toxic as any drug. Indulged without restraint, it causes untold wreckage to lives and relationships. When swallowed out of fear, it becomes a poison. It seeps into the body, making you depressed, nervous, and physically sick, and leaks out in passive-aggressive behavior.

I prefer to call anger a difficult emotion because of the intensity of the energy it produces. The problem with anger is not in the feeling itself, which is natural, but in how it is expressed. It can be expressed beneficially in appropriately assertive behavior and in protesting injustice. Problems occur, however, when that energy is either under-controlled or over-controlled. Unchecked, it can result in aggressive, harmful behavior that destroys people and relationships. If internalized, it can wreak havoc with your body and emotions.

Anger is a natural energy that helps you to survive when handled with care, compassion, and wisdom. For example, if you feel bullied in a relationship, anger empowers you to set limits. However, that energy can also be allowed to build up to explosive levels and erupt in violent behavior towards yourself and others. You may feel possessed by the demon anger and powerless to channel that energy in wholesome ways. You become preoccupied with the wrongs done to you and dwell on revenge. You doubt you can resist striking out at those who treated you unfairly. Enemies appear everywhere as the anger takes over your psyche. When your anger becomes excessive, you feel out of control.

The frequency of road rage signals the overpowering presence of anger in our culture and in ourselves. One woman related to me, "My daughter just started driving. I told her to just look ahead at stop lights. If you make eye contact, you may invite trouble."

While there is no formal diagnosis of an anger disorder, the hostile mood accompanies many other clinical diagnoses. Nearly half of those who are depressed develop an irritable mood. Depression has been described as "anger turned inward," because it often results in harsh self-criticism and suicidal violence. Many suffering from anxiety lash out at others when their routines are upset or they are forced out of their comfort zones. Eighty percent of those diagnosed with bipolar disorder become irritable when manic. Aggressive behavior is also frequent. Resentment is a driving force in addiction to alcohol and drugs. Many alcoholics and drug addicts become angry and violent when under the influence (1).

Even though you may not be diagnosed with an anger disorder, you may believe you have an anger sickness. The fire of rage may burn in you, and you feel powerless to extinguish it. You may see yourself as a "rageholic" or "grudgeholic." Your anger may take on an addictive quality. You both love and hate being intoxicated with it. One patient admitted to me, "My anger gives me a rush that exhilarates me for a minute—and then it turns against me." If you wonder if you are addicted to anger, ask yourself the following questions:

- Do you often feel overwhelmed by your aggressive impulses and unable to control your temper?

- Do you consider your anger excessive, even crippling at times?

- Do you feel a secret pleasure in the sense of power your anger gives you?

- Does your preoccupation with the unfairness of life and being wronged interfere with your happiness?

- Does your need for power and control seem excessive, interfering with your relationships?

- Has your life become unmanageable because of your anger?

- Do you feel hopeless about finding a cure for your anger?

You may discover, if you are honest with yourself, that you both love and hate your anger. On the one hand, it gives you an adrenaline rush and you feel momentarily powerful. You take pleasure in standing up for yourself, telling people off, or intimidating others to do your bidding. Revenge can feel sweet. On the other hand, after your aggressive displays, you feel shame and guilt for your behavior. You hate being out of control. The broken relationships and the hurt you cause those you love make you grieve. Anger can act like a stimulant drug that energizes you and causes you to act insane. "Mad" and "madness" share the same root word.

You may think of addiction only as a chemical dependency on substances like alcohol, drugs, or nicotine. You may even consider some compulsive behaviors, like gambling, shopping, and over-eating or over-sexing, addictive. Nevertheless, mood states and habits of thinking can also possess an addictive quality. For example, anxiety, fear, and worry may act like a stimulant drug. You become preoccupied with the dangers in life, worst-case scenarios, and a sense of helplessness, so you withdraw from life into a safety zone. Sadness and a depressed mood may simulate a sedative-hypnotic, causing you to sleepwalk through life. You focus on past painful losses and disengage from the present. You can become stuck in these moods and ways of thinking, powerless to extricate yourself (2).

As helpless as you feel in the grip of anger and hatred, there is a way out. Your desperate sense of hopelessness can be a prelude to new life.

Steps to a New Life

The most effective recovery program for the many forms of addiction, including anger, was born in the United States—the fellowship of Alcoholics Anonymous. It is a distinctively American technology for healing, growth, and leading a better life. Initially begun by Bill Wilson for alcoholics, its approach to addictive behavior has been so successful that those with a host of other problems, such as gambling, sex addiction, and over-eating, have benefited from working the program. Its practical wisdom can help anyone serious about personal growth, not only those with emotional and behavioral disturbances.

While uniquely American, the Twelve Steps of AA also has a universal appeal because it is rooted in common-sense human wisdom. Grown in our native soil, it is a flowering of seeds planted from the beginning of our history as a nation. What is so American about this program? AA is built on the following values:

Rugged Individualism. Our pilgrim predecessors sailed across the ocean to the new world on a quest for freedom. They wanted independence from the political-religious establishment that persecuted them. They left their familiar home to begin a new life. They affirmed the dignity of the human person. Looking inward and trusting their own experience, they undertook a courageous journey. Questioning their inherited traditions, they took personal responsibility to build a new life for themselves.

Alcoholics Anonymous encourages its members to take responsibility for their own lives, not blaming others, and to seek freedom from their oppressive addictions. Just as the Lone Ranger had Tonto, the program also emphasizes the need for companionship on the soul-searching journey of recovery. AA is a fellowship of rugged individuals who walk the road less travelled.

Moral Idealism. Our ancestors came to found a nation that promised liberty and justice for all. Contrary to the monarchy of their homeland, they established a democracy in which all would have a voice in the government. Our Puritan founders were deeply religious and wanted all to exercise freedom of conscience in choosing their own beliefs. They undertook an "errand into the wilderness" and saw themselves as missionaries bringing their faith to the Promised Land.

The AA program is spiritual without aligning with any religious denomination. It invites its members to look inward, discover their own Higher Power, and live a value-directed life.

Practical Action. We Americans are impatient with idle speculation. We are a people of action who set goals, plan strategies, and get results. Our ancestors taught us to work hard to achieve our goals. We want a better life now, and not just in the afterlife. We are willing to try new technologies to improve the world and our lives.

Alcoholics Anonymous encourages that enterprising spirit. It offers practical wisdom and insists that its members actively work the program. Diligently working the program, with the help of God, promises results.

Pioneering Spirit. Our pilgrim ancestors left the security of their homeland and undertook a perilous voyage to an unknown land. They built a new home for themselves, but they did not settle down. Their curiosity and courage drove them to explore unfamiliar territory to the west. An adventurous spirit possessed them. They did not rest with convention, but displayed minds and hearts open to the new.

The steps of AA defy conventional wisdom as a path to healing and growth. They propose an upside-down therapy, a surprising path to recovery. However, upon deeper reflection they reveal an ageless wisdom, a trustworthy guide to the good life. The Twelve Steps can be summarized in four leaps of faith beyond ordinary expectations:

- Embrace the discomfort of your anger and learn its message. Don't try simply to control or get rid of it.

- Trust in your Higher Power. Expand your ordinary consciousness.

- Your anger is not the problem, only a symptom of the problem. It reveals where you may be stuck in life. Explore and remove the character defects it shows.

- Help yourself by helping others. Move from an anger-driven life to a value-directed one.

Working the steps leads you to the antidote to anger—forgiveness. Forgiveness is a process that involves letting go of your anger and your desire for revenge against those who wronged you. It also requires transforming the energy of your anger into compassion and kindness.

The word forgiveness (fore-give) means, "to give ahead of time." As giving, it is an act of generosity, a gift. Given ahead of time, it is offered before it is deserved or earned by the offending party. You forgive for your own sake, to free yourself from bondage to your wrath. The miracle of forgiveness is that you are healed by extending yourself to the one who harmed you.

How to Use This Book

This book is divided into two parts. The first four chapters of part one describe what anger looks like, its similarity to addiction, how it develops, and how it shapes the personality. The second part presents an overview of the Twelve Steps and how each of the steps can be used as a practical guide to recovering from and growing through anger. Practices are offered as recovery aids. The case examples are composites of the stories of various patients, with details changed sufficiently to protect their confidentiality.

The Twelve Steps arose from a group experience. Bill Wilson consulted with many others, formed support groups, and refined the steps. The steps were formulated from the experience of alcoholics who gathered with a common goal, to become sober and improve their lives. They gathered in small groups to share their life experiences and work the steps. Within the fellowship they found support, understanding, and hope.

Anger is often treated in a group setting, such as anger management classes or therapy groups. You cannot heal from your addiction to anger alone. You need the support and encouragement of others on this perilous journey. I recommend that you use this book, not alone, but with at least one companion. It may be a therapist, a spouse, a close friend, or another who also struggles with anger. For example, I have several patients who use the exercises in the book and talk about what they learn in sessions. You need good company to succeed.

You may decide to join a support group. Many anger management groups focus on learning to control your anger. I suggest you view anger as your friend, not your enemy, and learn to listen to its wisdom. You may seek out a group like Emotions Anonymous, which uses the Twelve Steps as a guide for working through and learning from various emotional struggles, including anger.

My dream is that groups emerge that use the Twelve Steps specifically for developing a healthy relationship with anger. I would call them Anger Anonymous groups. You may feel inspired to gather a self-help group yourself. You are not alone in your suffering.

If you choose not to join with others, you can benefit from working with this book alone and using the exercises at the end of the chapters to aid in your own recovery. The steps need to be worked, not just thought about. For personal transformation, they must become a daily practice. Habits, which can prove stubborn, require concerted effort to be changed.

Family members can also benefit from this book. They can come to understand and accept their own sense of powerlessness to overcome the anger addiction of their loved ones. They need to resist being pulled into your anger and becoming anger addicted themselves.

Mental health professionals who treat angry patients may benefit from the book's presentation of a new way to think about anger and its treatment.

Clergy and religious authorities may appreciate the book's suggestions that a spiritual outlook and practice can enhance psychological wellbeing. It may provide them with a new way of looking at spirituality, presented in contemporary, this-worldly language.

At the heart of the anger addiction is the desire for control and power. Being out of control, not getting what you want, is the cause of your suffering. Anger arises from your unfulfilled expectations. It gives you a temporary feeling of power when you really feel helpless. As you work the steps, you will gain a different perspective on power, as expressed in *Tao Te Ching* (3):

> The Master's power is like this.
> He lets all things come and go
> effortlessly without desire.
> He never expects results;
> thus he is never disappointed.
> He is never disappointed;
> thus his spirit never grows old (55).

A mind rejecting reality fuels anger. My wish is that this book may aid you in surrendering to the abundance already present in your life. Living with calm acceptance and gratitude is the way to a joyful life.

Dennis Ortman, Ph.D.

PART ONE:
ANGER AS AN ADDICTION

Dennis Ortman, Ph.D.

1

Anger Styles:
Tending the Fire

"Anger's my meat. I sup upon myself and so shall starve with feeding."

—William Shakespeare

Everybody gets angry. "But not me," I told myself. In my father's drunken rages, I witnessed the devastating effects of uncontrolled anger. I saw dealing with anger as playing with fire. I could easily get burned. I decided at a young age, without really making a conscious choice, to smother any smoking tinders of irritation I felt. In remaining calm and controlled, I found safety and, I believed, acceptance and admiration from others. It was only many years later that I began to recognize the awful price I paid for my pseudo-tranquility.

Anger, a Powerful Energy

Anger is a natural energy, like fire. Our earliest ancestors witnessed the power of fire in lightning storms and raging forest fires. They also enjoyed the light and warmth it provided in their cold, dark world. It was like a god to them. They feared and worshiped it. They observed fire closely and came to appreciate its many forms and varying intensity, from a tiny flame to a roaring firestorm. They longed to find a way to harness and use its power for their benefit. Then, one day, some unknown caveman learned fire's secret and how to start, stop, control, and use it. Life changed dramatically.

We spend a lifetime learning to manage the fire of anger that burns in each of us. Its power fascinates, seduces, and frightens us. We both love and hate it. Anger takes on different meanings for each of us. Some of us like our angry emotions because they make us feel hot and alive. They mean we possess power and control. Others hate them because they makes us feel cold and empty. The emotion means we are powerless over ourselves and have lost control.

All of us seek to understand the secret of the power of this confusing and difficult emotion. By its nature, anger wants to defend, fight, and attack. We observe how it often begins with a subtle irritation, proceeds to an increased frustration and annoyance, and can become a rage and fury. The emotion can consume us, block clear thinking, and provoke irrational behavior. We long to discover ways to harness this energy.

If we are fortunate, we learn the immense benefits of anger well-managed. Anger is a natural stress response to a perceived danger, like fear. It serves a survival purpose. Darwin observed the savagery of nature, that only the fittest survived. Evolution advanced by the various species fighting for their lives. Like our ancestors in the animal world, in the face of danger, we instinctively fight, flee, or freeze. It is an automatic response, hard-wired into our brains and bodies. The intense emotional reaction to threat launches us into defensive action. We have a natural impulse to fight for our wellbeing.

For us humans with our developed consciousness, however, anger has many levels of meaning. Threats can be to both our physical and psychological wellbeing. Anger signals that something is wrong, that some important need is not being met, that a boundary is being violated, or that we are being treated unfairly. We experience a loss of wholeness. Like all the emotions, which are natural tendencies to action, anger motivates and energizes us to protect ourselves and protest against injustice. It is a power boost to assert ourselves in a world that can be threatening. When we use the energy of anger wisely, we gain a sense of self-esteem and self-control. Then it becomes a natural energy for personal change and growth.

All of us learn, from childhood and throughout adulthood, how to work with the fiery energy of anger. We develop our own unique styles that reflect our personality and temperament. A healthy, assertive style finds a balance between indulging and inhibiting this emotion. We know when, where, to whom, and how to express our anger effectively to achieve our goals. However, many of us lose a sense of balance and operate in the extremes. We may either under-control or over-control our aggressive impulses. The anger masters us, rather than the other way around.

The following are some examples of those who allow their anger to rage out of control. Rage rules them. Allowing their hostile impulses to go unchecked, they harm themselves and others. While they hate the harm done, they may love the feeling of power, control, and intimidation of others. Nevertheless, their lives become chaotic, risk-filled, and crisis-creating.

Rageholic

Martin, a former Marine with a temper:

> *"I've had a temper my whole life. People called me a hothead. But I also prided myself as a man of discipline. However, anger was always simmering below the surface, and I had to be on constant guard to keep it from erupting. That has been my most difficult challenge in life. Anything can set me off—someone looking at me funny or disrespecting me. I react instantly, without thinking. My temper has gotten me into*

a lot of trouble. I've been in many fights and spoiled relationships. I don't look for trouble, but I refuse to back down. I stand up for myself, and some people don't like that.

I realize that I am a lot like my father who had a terrible temper. He used to beat us kids for the smallest infractions. I felt bullied by him. I promised that I would never let anyone bully me again. My parents fought all the time. Our home was like a battlefield. I learned that only the fittest survive. Fortunately, I am a survivor. Now my toughest battle is with myself, with my temper."

Rachel, a complaining housewife:

"I was raised with high expectations. My mother taught me, 'Anything worth doing is worth doing right.' She was unbending with her demands. I raise my children to be the best they can be. I admit that sometimes I take it too far, and I nag them and my husband. Unlike my mother, though, I learned to control my temper. It takes a long time before I explode. I tell my family what I don't like in a calm voice. It's only when they don't listen that I begin to yell to get their attention."

Anger can be, for some, like a boiling pot of water. It may simmer for a while and suddenly boil over. Every now and then rageholics have to let off steam. Some come to a slow boil, while others become over-heated quickly. Depending on the sensitivity of the person, different experiences may stoke their fire. For example, some react to perceived disrespect, unfairness, or unmet expectations. They react differently in expressing their anger. Some become verbally aggressive with complaining, criticizing, or blaming. Others display their temper in physical violence. Still others keep their hostile thoughts to themselves. Harsh judgments constantly occupy their minds. The boiling anger within burns them, and the steam scalds others.

Grudgeholic

Lana, a betrayed woman:

"My husband had an affair with a coworker five years after we were married. That was twenty years ago. We stayed together for the sake of the children. He ended the affair, apologized profusely, and tried to make up for it with me, but I was devastated. How could he do that to me? I trusted him with my life. I never believed he could have done such a thing. Even today it seems unreal. A day never goes by that I don't think about the betrayal, and the anger rises in me. I still ask him questions about his lover, and he gets annoyed. It's only reassurance I'm asking for. I don't think he realizes how much it still hurts. I don't know if I'll ever be able to fully trust him again.

I'm very sensitive. I bruise easily. I keep a journal and carefully write down when people offend me. I need to protect myself. When the hurts reach a certain point, I ask myself if the relationship is really worth it. I may then decide I'm done. There are some relatives and friends I haven't spoken to in years. I can't tolerate being in their presence. It's just too painful."

The flames of hostility can burn for a long time. Some people are slow to anger, but once they reach the point of fury, they hang on to it. They are slow to forgive and forget. They come to identify the offending party as "the enemy." They believe that the persisting anger forms a protective wall around them.

However, resentment, literally the continuous re-feeling of the feeling, grows like an inner sore. They may accumulate grievances like small stones in a coat with many pockets. When they feel overburdened by the load, they dump it with an explosion of temper and end the relationship. These wound collectors never allow themselves to heal. Bitterness salts the wound. Their lives become organized around the pain, isolating them with feelings of self-pity. Joy eludes them.

The following are examples of those whose anger is over-controlled. Out of fear or shame, they suppress their powerful aggressive impulses. Detached from the energy of anger, they disconnect from their own sense of power and many other emotions. Their lives become rigid, empty, dependent, and emotionally starved. However, anger is too powerful a force to be bottled up completely. Despite their strained efforts to stuff their anger, it still seeps into their psyche and leaks out into their relationships. I personally felt exhausted holding my anger in. I didn't know why I was so tired, and probably depressed.

Silent Submission

Laura, an unhappily married woman:

"I married the love of my life. I admired my husband's strength and self-confidence. He was a man who was comfortable speaking up and taking charge in any situation. I let him take charge of the household and of me. It never bothered me for a long time, but things changed when the children were born. I felt so responsible for them and threw myself into being a mother. My husband objected to all the attention I gave them. He felt ignored, so he became more and more demanding of me. I went along for many years and honored his wishes. I ignored how torn I felt. I never spoke up for myself because I hate conflict so much. Now I feel so unhappy and lost. I don't know what I really want. I'm afraid if I don't do what he wants he will leave me. Then I will be all alone."

Some extinguish the life-giving energy of anger in their lives. They want to avoid conflict at all costs. They imagine that disagreements inevitably lead to arguments and eventually to an end of the relationship. Instead of speaking up for themselves, they pretend to agree. They have trouble saying no. They want peace. However, the conflict they avoid with others is internalized. They are not at peace with themselves. Furthermore, because they have submerged so much of themselves, they may not even know what they think or feel. They lose themselves and begin to feel dead inside.

Those who suppress their anger may fear its power because they witnessed its devastating effects when out of control in childhood. To compensate, they choose the opposite, to exert excessive control. They deny, suppress, and stuff their anger, along with any other uncomfortable feelings. The result is feeling disengaged from themselves and life. The stifled anger attacks their spirit. They feel empty, powerless, and dead.

To self-medicate the discomfort of hostile feelings, many turn to alcohol and drugs. They are particularly drawn to pain-relieving drugs, such as opiates. Our society encourages high expectations and the aggressive pursuit of them. It is no coincidence that we are experiencing an epidemic of opiate abuse to calm our frustrated strivings. Many begin using opiates for physical pain and abuse them to medicate emotional pain. Soon the drug takes over their lives and drains their energy.

Depression

Leo, a grief-stricken man:

"After my wife died, I attended a support group. I couldn't understand why so many of the people talked about how angry they were about their loved ones dying. I only felt grief and guilt. I tell myself I could have done more to keep her from getting sick and dying. My wife is now deceased three years, and I am still depressed. My children try to comfort me, but I don't want to burden them. I just keep going on with little joy in my life. I'm impatient with myself that I can't get over my grief. My whole life I felt like I was not good enough. I couldn't please my parents. I felt like a failure on the job. My kids got into trouble, and I blamed myself. Now I can't get my life together since my wife died. What's wrong with me?"

Russell, a perfectionist:

"I work as an engineer at a large corporation. I've been there 15 years. Whenever cuts are made at work, I'm terrified I'll be laid off. I live with almost constant dread that I'm not doing a good enough job and will be fired. I push myself hard at work and in everything I do. People tell me I'm a perfectionist because I have such high standards. They're right. I take pride in those standards. But I never feel like I live up to them. I feel so much pressure to prove myself. It's so depressing because I cannot relax with any of my successes. It's a never-ending battle that exhausts me."

The flame of anger can be directed inward when it is not fully acknowledged or expressed. Another name for depression is "anger turned inward." Instead of admitting anger and fighting for themselves in a difficult situation, those who become depressed feel helpless and blame themselves. They become self-critical of their own weaknesses. As one woman stated, "I live under a mountain of self-reproach." She was afraid of standing up for herself and hated herself for her cowardice. The extreme of turning the violence of anger against oneself, of course, is suicide.

Another name for depression is "learned helplessness." Those prone to depression entertain high expectations of themselves and others and are frequently disappointed. However, instead of blaming others, they direct their aggression against themselves in self-blame. They judge themselves mercilessly for not being perfect. Of course, perfection is impossible. Those depressed may even acknowledge the impossibility of reaching their standards. However, they stubbornly refuse to lower their standards and live with an unrelenting sense of failure and helplessness. Their suppressed anger attacks their emotional wellbeing.

Medical Problems

Reggie, experiencing back pain:

"I've suffered from back pain for years. Sometimes it is so crippling I can't function. I don't recall injuring my back on the job or anywhere else. All of a sudden, for some unknown reason, I felt excruciating pain in my back. I've gone to countless doctors over the years and received little relief. They told me I have a mildly bulging disk, but it does not explain the level of pain. They also tell me how tense I seem. I've tried medications, physical therapy, and chiropractors. Now I'm suspecting an emotional component to the pain and reading books on how suppressing anger causes such pain. In therapy, I'm realizing how tense I've always felt and how judgmental I am about myself and others. I've been that way my whole life."

Melinda, unable to relax:

"I've been uptight, unable to relax, my whole life. Everything stresses me out. I hate my job, but cannot leave it. I fight with my husband, but am afraid to be on my own. I feel trapped. My childhood was stressful, with my alcoholic father who yelled all the time and my mother who criticized me constantly. I felt so tense growing up. No wonder I never learned to relax. Now I'm having stomach problems, acid reflux and possible ulcers. I grind my teeth at night and wear a mouth-guard. I also have a ringing in my ears that the doctors can find no medical cause for. They tell me it might be related to the constant tension I feel in my neck and shoulders."

If the energy of anger is not allowed to flow naturally through the body, it can cause damage. When we swallow anger, it becomes a bitter pill, hard to digest. The fight-or-flight response, with no outlet, targets the body. Research has shown that excessive cortisol levels, which result from unremitting stress, lower the immune system. The body then becomes vulnerable to a variety of diseases. Aches and pains develop, particularly in the back and neck, with the increased muscle tension. Suppressed anger also can result in increased risks for high blood pressure, heart attacks, gastric problems, ulcers, and even cancer. Stifled anger attacks the body and can be life-threatening.

Our bodies have a wisdom that the mind does not grasp. Emotions arise from spontaneous physical reactions to events. The body also holds tension from the strain of our interacting with the world. That tension resides within the body for a lifetime. It is not relieved until we recognize it and learn to release the tension. The body talks. Are we attuned to its message?

Silent Treatment

Elaine, estranged from her family:

"Growing up, my mother was depressed and criticized me mercilessly. I could never please her. When I was old enough to move out, I left home. I was so angry that I never wanted to see her again. She tried to contact me countless times, but I refused to talk with her. I just lived my own life, felt sorry for myself, and complained about her to anyone who would listen. When she was sick and dying, I relented and went to see her. She apologized for being so hard on me growing up, and I was over-whelmed with guilt. I realized how I pushed away everyone who ever hurt me. I was stubborn and made excuses. I ended up living a very lonely life."

Anger is not only hot, involving fireworks. It can also be the cold anger of emotional withdrawal, creating a hostile atmosphere like the cold war between the United States and Russia. All friendliness disappears. Those who engage in passive-aggressive behavior avoid any direct confrontation. They do not fully admit the depth of rage to themselves. They do not even tell the offending party how hurt and angry they feel. Instead, they construct an impenetrable wall. They bob and weave, fail to follow through, speak indirectly, and manipulate. All these behaviors provoke anger in others. They keep themselves at a safe and lonely distance from others.

Paranoid

Albert, not trusting anyone:

"I don't trust anyone. I've been married and divorced three times. Each time, my wife became my enemy and we battled constantly. I have to admit that I'm always on my guard in relationships, with friends and in business. It's a dog-eat-dog world, and people are only looking out for themselves. They will take advantage of you if you let them. 'Fool me once, shame on you; fool me twice, shame on me.' So I watch my back. I'm alert and careful.

I learned from my father not to trust anyone. He was a cutthroat businessman. He owned his own business and always drove a hard bargain. No one cheated him. At home, he was just as tough. He ruled with an iron fist. Any disobedience, talking back, or sign of disrespect was met with the belt. I hated it, but I saw the wisdom of his approach."

Rebecca, suspicious of her husband:

"I'm convinced my husband is having an affair with my best friend. He insists he is not, and we argue about it all the time. I can tell just by the way they look at each other. I don't have any proof—yet. But I keep looking. I check his phone and emails all the time. That infuriates him. Whenever he comes home late from work,

I suspect he was with her. I confront him, and we argue. My father had affairs my mother never knew about. I'll never allow myself to be humiliated like she was."

Some, consumed by an unacknowledged anger, see the world as a threatening place. They see challenges everywhere and feel compelled to protect themselves. Especially if they are out of touch with their own anger, they are acutely sensitive to the hostility of others. They frequently see others as mad at them, even when there is no evidence of it. Those with paranoid tendencies use a defense mechanism called projection. They project what they feel inside onto the outer world, as if on a movie screen. For them, their projections are real. If they are angry, they believe they live in a hostile world. They see enemies everywhere.

Since their projections are real for them, the image they create of the world guides their actions. Since they view the world as a dangerous place, they feel compelled to act defensively. They may believe that the best defense is a good offense and attack others before they are attacked. However, that defensiveness has consequences. It provokes the hostility they fear from others. They feel treated unfairly, and react defensively. A cycle of hostility is created, each accusing the other of being unfair. Each will see themselves as a victim in need of protection. Their anger provides the means to protect themselves, and thus fuels the cycle.

We spend a lifetime coming to terms with the powerful, frightening energy of anger within us. How we cope shapes our personalities. The styles of coping described above overlap at many points. During our lifetimes and in different situations, our styles change and develop. However, most of us cling to one particular style, with only minor variations.

Our life task will be to recognize our tendencies, understand their strengths and weaknesses, and learn to find balance. The first step will be in recognizing our preferred style. The sooner we work with it, the quicker we can free ourselves from its grasp and avoid becoming addicted to the power and control anger offers.

2

Addicted to Anger:
An Instinct Run Wild

"Anger, with its poisoned source and fevered climax, murderously sweet,
that you must slay to weep no more."

—Buddha

AA cautions that alcohol is "cunning, baffling, powerful." That also applies to anger. I imagined that I was immune from the ravages of anger because I had suppressed it so effectively. Unlike my father, I thought I had it under control. I had become such an expert at stuffing my feelings that I became like a ball bearing rolling through life. I was resilient. Nothing seemed to upset me. I kept a calm exterior. I had anger beat.

My bubble burst when I noticed a sense of emptiness, a depressed mood, seeped into my life. Everything was going so well, according to plan. I graduated college with honors. I completed my theology studies in Rome. I was about to fulfill my lifelong dream to be ordained a priest. But something was not right. "I have no reason to be depressed," I told myself. At the advice of my spiritual director, I began therapy. Between sessions, after painful memories emerged, I took long walks alone. I recall the distinct feeling that there was a volcano inside me about to erupt. It terrified me. I had no idea what terrible things would emerge. I was not in control and felt powerless.

Out of Balance

AA describes alcoholism as "instincts run wild." Alcoholics lose the capacity to drink in moderation. Urges to drink come fast and furious. The alcoholic feels powerless to resist. After taking the first drink, he does not know when he will stop. Even if he has made a firm resolution to stop and has been sober for a long time, one drink will cause him to lose his balance. He falls off the wagon.

Under the influence of alcohol, he often loses control of his thoughts, emotions, and behavior. Alcohol is a "dis-inhibitor." It turns off the brakes in the brain. Alcoholics often careen out of control and lose balance in their lives. Their tempers rage. They say silly and hurtful things to loved ones and friends. Their thinking is scattered, confused, and irrational. They show poor judgment in making decisions and act in ways that would embarrass them when sober.

Like drinking in moderation, the healthy, balanced expression of anger is beneficial. The energy of anger enables us to express ourselves freely, to stand up for ourselves, and to establish appropriate boundaries. It enables us to protect ourselves against threats. Expressing anger appropriately increases our sense of personal power and self-esteem.

For example, I was a college student in Detroit during the 1967 riots. Our college was just a few blocks from where the burning began. A couple of my professors were outraged at what was happening, the burning, shooting, and rioting that revealed a heinous racial prejudice. They started a program called Focus Hope to help poor blacks and raise consciousness. In the spirit of Martin Luther King, they initiated peaceful demonstrations. I joined in. People of all colors walked together, linked arms, and sang, "We shall overcome." That was a balanced, beneficial response to the racial violence on the part of some, and the uncaring passivity of others.

However, anger can become an "instinct run wild" if its energy is not used with wisdom and compassion. Like a wild stallion without a skillful rider, it can run rampant. The rider falls off and is trampled. Bystanders can be injured. Under the influence of uncontrolled anger, our lives also become unbalanced. We harm ourselves and those we love, saying, doing, and thinking things outside the realm of reason.

Unlike alcohol, though, we cannot live without anger, which is a natural instinct. We can also suffer from too little anger. Our lives become out of balance when our aggressive impulses are over-controlled. It is like a lively stallion fenced in a tiny corral. The untamed instinct that corrals the natural energy may be fear or shame. The stifled anger wants to run free or be harnessed for some useful purpose, but the caged anger thrashes about, wildly discharging its energy against the helpless rider, and injuring him emotionally and physically. The anger also spills out unknowingly in our relationships, causing hurt and distance.

The experience of unbalanced anger parallels that of addiction to alcohol and other drugs. The following are characteristics of both anger and addiction:

- Excessive: too much, too little.

- Denial of harm.

- Preoccupation and repetition: going in circles.

- Loss of control: passion's slave.

- Will to power: a control freak.

- Self-medicating the pain of life.

- Beyond cure: feeling powerless.

Let me briefly explain how the experience of the alcoholic, as an example of an addicted person, overlaps with what you experience with unbalanced anger.

Excessive: Too Much, Too Little

Drinking with friends is a normal pleasure for many people. Alcohol helps them relax, let down their hair, and talk freely in social situations. It is a natural tranquilizer used as a social lubricant. Drinking has become so much a part of our culture that the effort to stop it during the Prohibition failed. "We want our beer!" placards were carried by protesters in a picture from an anti-Prohibition rally I saw recently.

Social drinking presents no problems until it increases, often imperceptibly, and crosses an invisible line to become alcoholic drinking. The reasons for consuming alcohol, often unconscious, shift from drinking for pleasure to drinking to feel normal. Alcoholics then want to drink to avoid the hangovers and shakes. They need to drink more and more just to feel normal. They manufacture excuses for their need to drink. At this point, the AA slogan applies, "One drink is too much, and a thousand is not enough." Anger, too, can become excessive.

William, suffering road rage:

> "My wife tells me I become a madman driving a car. I can't believe how stupid some drivers are—and dangerous. They weave in and out of traffic and cut you off. It infuriates me, especially when someone cuts in front of me. I honk my horn, scream at them, and give them the finger. I just want to let them know how stupid they are. Sometimes I become so enraged that I tailgate them for miles. I think to myself, if they ever stop, I'll get out of my car and beat the crap out of them. My wife says I'm so crazy behind the wheel that she refuses to drive with me."

You can live without alcohol or drugs, but not without anger. It is always there as a natural reaction to perceived threat. You just need to learn to handle it well. Problems occur with anger at the extremes, as with fire. Without fire, we live in a cold, dark world. However, if the fire of anger rages out of control, it can ravage your life. Under the influence of indulged anger, you lose the ability to think clearly and make rational judgments. You strike out at those you love and at innocent parties, imagining them as your enemies. You may become violent toward yourself and others. Your life becomes chaotic and full of self-created crises. Afterwards, shame follows you like a dark cloud.

Jerry, a compliant husband:

> "My wife regularly gives me to-do lists. Sometimes I don't mind it, but other times I just don't want to do it. I rarely speak up. When I've objected in the past, she flies into a rage. She calls me lazy and irresponsible. Her anger terrifies me, so I just keep quiet and go along to keep the peace. But I don't feel good inside. I hate that I'm so afraid of her and let her dominate me. I've lost respect for myself. I feel like such a coward."

At the other extreme, in suppressing your anger, you make yourself a victim. You cut yourself off from your natural power source, making yourself weak and defenseless. Then, your anxiety increases. The world becomes a threatening place. You may withdraw from activities to keep yourself safe. Your world shrinks. Fear keeps you from asserting yourself and pursuing your desires, especially if you perceive any opposition. Relinquishing your own natural power, you lose respect for yourself, and others respect you less. You begin to feel lifeless and empty. Instead of using your anger to be assertive, you direct it against yourself. You may become depressed, self-critical, and have many somatic complaints.

Both addictions and anger sicknesses are marked by excess. While drinking becomes a problem when too much is consumed regularly, anger can cause harm when it is excessively indulged or suppressed. Life may become either chaotic or empty. Addictive behaviors may reach a point in their excess that the pain is barely tolerable. You only want relief. Paradoxically, embracing that pain can move you to seek help and eventual recovery.

Denial of Harm

Alcoholics live in denial about their drinking, which allows the chaos and confusion to continue. They suffer from a disease of perception. They cannot add correctly, insisting that they had only "a couple drinks," while their loved ones come to a different total. Their memory is selective. Alcoholics seem to remember only the good times drinking and forget the hangovers and obnoxious behavior while drunk. They recall the drink and not the drunk. They are also masters at rationalizing. Alcoholics can give you a million reasons why they need to drink, saying with complete conviction, "I drink because I'm happy, sad, stressed, or just enjoy the taste." In their selective awareness, they overlook the obvious harm they cause themselves and others.

The consequences of the denial can be catastrophic. Drunkenness leads to accidents, failed marriages, lost jobs, and premature death. It allows the illness to progress and go untreated. The result, as AA bluntly puts it, is "insanity or death." Similarly, the harm of anger is often rationalized.

Larry, a man with regular temper outbursts, told me, "My daughter called to tell me she caught her husband cheating on her. I was infuriated and wanted to kill him. I told her I would find him and beat the crap out of him. I wanted to protect her."

"How would that protect her? The deed is already done," I pointed out.

"I would teach him a lesson, never to do it again," he reasoned.

"And what would happen to you?" I asked.

"I'd probably end up in jail, but I would have sweet revenge," he said proudly.

"And for how long do you think it would feel sweet?" I enquired.

"I really wouldn't care," he said.

Genevieve, a woman who hides her anger:

> *"My parents told me, 'Anger is the work of the devil.' They were strict born-again Christians. I believed what they said and swallowed my anger. My parents taught us what was right and wrong, had firm rules, and punished us with the belt when we broke them. We got what we deserved. I became a very obedient child and never talked back. I tried to stay invisible. Sometimes when I felt anger as a teen, I cut myself with a razor blade. It helped me to control myself and gave me some relief."*

The word "mad" shares the same root word as "madness." Anger, in the extremes, can distort your perceptions and thinking. If you have temper outbursts, you may rationalize that you are not really hurting anyone, including yourself. The storm passes, and sunshine returns. You imagine that others learn to ignore your outbursts and let them pass without a thought, just like you do. However, the effects of your anger flashes may linger and alienate them from you, and cost you dearly.

If you hold onto or suppress your anger without expressing it directly, you may imagine you are not hurting anyone. "If they don't know, it can't hurt them," you tell yourself. Furthermore, you may not see the harmful impact of your swallowed rage on your body and mood. You fail to see the connection between your denied feelings and your aches, pains, medical problems, depression, and low self-esteem.

You may not recognize it, but anger, whether indulged or suppressed, mostly hurts you. As AA astutely observes, "Being angry is like consuming rat poison and expecting the rat to die."

Both the addicted and the angry ignore the warning signs from their bodies, their families, and their friends who know they have a problem. They suffer a case of distorted perception. Their sense of shame keeps them in denial. Tragically, their denial will prolong the suffering unnecessarily. It will keep them from getting help for conditions that are very treatable.

Preoccupation and Repetition: Going in Circles

Alcoholics are stuck in "stinking thinking" and irrational behavior. They develop many strange ideas about alcohol, such as, "I can't live without it." They come to believe that they will find happiness in a bottle, that drinking will magically erase all their problems. They think they need to drink when they are happy, sad, anxious, or angry. In other words, whenever they feel anything. Their awareness becomes suspiciously selective. With "euphoric recall," they remember only the good times drinking and forget the trouble it caused. Their preoccupation is the next drink.

The obsessive thinking spills over into compulsive behaviors. Alcoholics develop bizarre rituals, rules, and routines around drinking. They proclaim, with unblinking assurance, that they cannot be alcoholic because they never drink alone, in the morning, all day, or every day. They begin to plan their days and social activities around alcohol consumption. They choose friends who drink just like them. Soon, without realizing it, alcohol becomes the organizing principle of their lives. It is their constant companion, and eventually, their only friend. Anger also can become an engrained habit of thinking and behaving.

Elizabeth, sensitive to being ignored:

> *"I've been angry with my husband for years of hurt and neglect. I feel like I raised our six children alone. He worked hard, but when he was home, he was busy with his projects and hobbies. He ignored me and the kids. I know he has ADHD, but that's no excuse for not paying attention to what needs to be done. When he ignores me, I feel a knot in my stomach. I can't help thinking about how little he cares. It hurts so much. I tell him what needs to be done, but he doesn't follow through. I end up screaming at him. He apologizes, does the job, but the same thing happens over and over again. I'm ready to tear my hair out."*

Consumed by anger, your thinking follows a single track. You obsess about how you were wronged and begin to think of the other person as your enemy. You become preoccupied with the hurt and outrage. Even though you may recognize that your dwelling on the hurt only harms you, you cannot stop yourself. To right the wrong, you may lash out at the offending party. That person may become defensive and retaliate, creating a vicious circle of hostility. You may know that the pattern of reacting is self-defeating, but, again, you cannot stop yourself. Over time, like water circling a drain, your life revolves around the perceived wound.

Both the anger addicted and the alcoholic go in circles with their minds and their behavior. Alcoholics obsess about the next drink, while the angry dwell on how they have been treated unfairly. Alcoholics develop rituals and routines, chasing the party for their next drink. Those who are angry become lost in their negative thoughts, plot revenge, and engage in never-ending fights. They remain stuck unless they fall on their faces onto the path of recovery.

Loss of Control: Passion's Slave

What makes someone an alcoholic is not how much or how often she drinks, but what happens when she drinks. The primary symptom is loss of control. When she drinks, she is not sure when she will stop. She may not lose control every time, but as the illness progresses, she becomes intoxicated more often. Because of her denial, she may believe she can stop whenever she likes. However, in her stubbornness, she ignores all the evidence to the contrary. She will only enter recovery when she fully acknowledges the reality, her powerlessness over alcohol.

As the illness progresses, the loss of control, with its devastating effects, deepens. The drinking takes over her life. An AA saying describes the decline accurately: "First, the man takes the drink; then, the drink takes the drink; and finally, the drink takes the man." Likewise, anger can become a harsh master.

Penelope, always fighting:

> *"Life has treated me unfairly, and I'm angry about it. I was born under the sign of Libra, which is constantly torn. My fate has been that I must fight for everything I want, but never get it. My parents fought all the time. My relationships have been battlefields, so I decided never to marry. I'm good at my job, but I was fired for reporting my boss for stealing from the company. No good deed goes unpunished.*

I have had more than my share of medical problems, ulcers, asthma, and a heart condition. I'm always angry. I hate it, but I feel helpless to get rid of it. I feel so empty inside without my anger, my constant companion. I'm afraid I would fall into despair if I let go of my anger."

Anger is "murderously sweet." You hold onto or hold in your anger because it benefits you in some way. It is high octane fuel that can make you feel powerful and energized when you feel helpless and weak. It gives you an adrenaline rush. You can use it to intimidate others and get your way, but soon the power of anger, when used unwisely, shows itself to be an illusion. You begin to feel helpless in its grip. Knowing that the anger poisons you and your relationships, you cannot escape its venomous effects. It starts to take over your life, interrupt your sleep, and enslave you.

The core of both unbalanced anger and addiction is the loss of control. At some level, both addicted and angry individuals realize that they are under the influence of a power greater than themselves, but they feel powerless to disengage. Both see themselves as helpless victims in life. Acknowledging their powerlessness can open the door to recovery.

Will to Power: a Control Freak

Alcoholics Anonymous describes alcoholics as people who are "self-centered in the extreme," and whose trouble is caused by "the misuse of willpower." Feeling so helpless, so out of control with his life, the alcoholic craves power and control. When he first begins drinking, the alcoholic discovers the magical quality of alcohol to transform his moods and personality. He enjoys the pleasurable feeling of intoxication and escaping painful reality. With time and experience, he finds in alcohol the means to control his mind, mood, and world, whenever he wants. Alcohol is his personal genie in a bottle.

For a time, alcohol is a wonder drug, the elixir of life—until the addiction takes hold. As his drinking increases, the miracle drug that freed him begins to control him. The instrument he used to master his world now enslaves him. Angry people, too, are power hungry and end up starving.

Fred, a hard-driving businessman:

"Success drives me. I'm a type-A personality. I always admired Donald Trump, a man who does not tolerate nonsense and is not afraid to speak his mind. At a young age, I started my own auto parts business. It's a competitive business, and I enjoy the challenge. I kept my business going when many others went under during the recession. I believe I'm successful because of the quality of my product. I hold myself and all my employees to the highest standards. I admit I get angry at times and yell and scream, but that is only to maintain a high level of performance. My family tells me I can be a bully and act like I'm at work, but I push them to be the best for their own good. One day they will thank me."

The craving for power and control often fuels anger. Bluntly expressing anger then becomes the instrument of control. Others bend to your will. You get what you want. You accomplish your goals. You may be intoxicated by its power for a period of time, until you realize the price you pay personally and in your relationships. Over time, the sustained angry reaction takes its toll on your emotions and physical wellbeing. You become hardened, incapable of the softer emotions of love, compassion, and joy. Unable to relax, your body begins to show the strain. Your anger does not draw people closer to you, but drives them away. Eventually, you are alone, sustained by the illusion of being a powerful person.

Both those in the grip of anger and alcoholics want the world to dance to their tune. They entertain dreams of how they imagine their lives should be and use their anger and alcohol to make it so, but sooner or later they have a collision with reality. They learn the limits of their control. When they can finally admit their powerlessness, their recovery can begin.

Self-Medicating the Pain of Life

Alcoholism arises from suffering and is a means to relieve suffering. Most alcoholics, contrary to popular belief, are sensitive souls searching for something more in life. They know, from bitter experience, that life is hard, and they look for some way to make it easier.

Imagine the joy when drinkers discover, in alcohol, a power greater than themselves to relieve them of their suffering and give them some momentary pleasure. They find in alcohol a medicine that acts more quickly, simply, and effectively than anything else they have tried. Alcohol is their natural, easily accessible tranquilizer that numbs the pain of life. It offers a quick fix, a magical cure. It allows them to withdraw from the hassles of life. When drinking, they are carefree and do not have a worry in the world. The nagging wife, the boring job, and the screaming kids can be forgotten in the moments of sweet intoxication. In a similar way, anger provides temporary relief.

Carolyn, angry at her alcoholic husband:

"I knew my husband had a drinking problem when I married him. It didn't matter to me because I loved him so much. I saw him as my soul mate, but over the years his drinking has gotten worse. He drinks every day. I would call him a happy drunk because he always wants to have fun. I envy his ability to relax. I can't. I'm super-responsible and take on more than I can handle at work and home. I yell and scream at my husband when he ignores things around the house that need to be done. I should probably leave him, but I feel addicted to him and love his charm. He reminds me of my father who drank and ran off with another woman. Our family fell apart when he left."

Clinging to your anger, as painful as it may be, can hide a deeper pain. As the Jewish advice goes, "Hit your head against the wall. When you stop you'll feel better." The anger can distract you from deeper, less tolerable pains in your life. For example, many bullies feel weak, frightened, and ashamed, but hide their discomfort by making others afraid of them. Trying to control others with your anger may help you avoid looking at what you need to change in your life. The anger may also cover over deep childhood wounds of being abandoned.

Avoidance is the middle name of both addicted and excessively angry persons. Both may be exquisitely sensitive people who have difficulty coping with life. Their drinking or hostility may disguise deep hurts. Easily overwhelmed, they develop survival strategies to maintain their wellbeing. They find relief from the unavoidable pain of life by numbing themselves with a drug or withdrawing into their resentments, but the pain inevitably breaks through, extending an invitation to recovery.

Beyond Cure: Feeling Powerless

Many alcoholics entertain a persistent fantasy that one day they will be able to drink like everyone else. Alcoholics Anonymous bursts their bubble, proclaiming, "Once an alcoholic, always an alcoholic." The program suggests that alcoholics have an allergy to alcohol and a disease for which there is no cure. However, there is a simple solution to the immediate problem: do not take a drink. "It's only the first drink you have to worry about," AA reminds it members.

It may take a while for an alcoholic to accept the reality of their condition. It usually takes many failed attempts at social drinking, several relapses, and a world of trouble before they accept the truth and admit, "I have an incurable illness called alcoholism." That awareness frees them from the hopeless struggle to control their drinking. When they learn to surrender, they can begin the work of recovery. Anger, too, can be a sickness that is hard to cure.

Angela, filled with self-hatred:

> *"I hate myself. I have nothing but contempt for myself. My mother praised my older sister for being smart and constantly reminded me of how stupid I was. I think she was right. I had trouble in school and barely make a living on my job. All my relationships have failed because I was stupid enough to choose losers. I think I'm so broken that I'm beyond repair. I have been in therapy several times and tried a bunch of different medications. Nothing worked. I feel so hopeless. I don't think anything will help. The only thing that keeps me from killing myself is how it would affect my little daughter."*

Which is worse, hatred of yourself or others? Both can be equally destructive and result in a violent loss of life. That hatred can become persistent and seem hopelessly incurable. You may label yourself a certified "hothead," despairing you can ever control your temper, or you may see yourself as chronically depressed. In both cases, you notice an ebb and a flow in your hostile mood. You feel occasional peace, but have relapses. The persistent thoughts of being wronged never leave. The desire to seek revenge on yourself or others never fades, so you stew in the juices of your anger. The black cloud of despair enshrouds you.

Anger, like any addiction, can take control of your life and not let go. You may despair of ever finding a cure. However, your sense of hopelessness to overcome it can launch you on a search for a new creative way for recovery. You can free yourself from the bondage to anger.

Dennis Ortman, Ph.D.

3

The Addictive Process:
The Pursuit of Power and Glory

"If a small thing has the power to make you angry,
does that not indicate something about your size?"

—Sydney Harris

Growing up with an alcoholic father, I felt powerless. I wanted to become invisible when my father came home late from the bar. I felt scared and helpless as the regular drama unfolded. Arriving home intoxicated, my father angrily demanded, "Where's my dinner?"

"We ate three hours ago. You're drunk again. That disgusts me," my mother boldly said.

Clenching his fists, my father shouted, "And you drive me to drink." I waited in fear for a physical fight to follow, which happened all too often.

At an early age, I devised a strategy to overcome my sense of helplessness. I entertained a fantasy to rescue myself and our family. I wanted to be a success. Even more, I wanted to be the best. I threw myself into my studies in school, was nearly an all-A student, and graduated college as valedictorian. I competed ferociously in sports, hating to lose. Ironically, in desiring to serve others, I pursued careers that offered power and glory as a priest and a psychologist. Some would praise this energetic pursuit of worthwhile goals. Our society encourages it. However, at some point, I realized its emptiness. I lost myself in the chase after success and praise.

Anger is a natural power, which can be either life-giving or destructive. Like the energy of the atom, anger's energy is highly explosive. If directed outward, it can change the world, for good or evil. If suppressed, it can ravage your insides. Even if you think you have it under control, the anger can leak out through indirect aggressive actions, as my life demonstrates. Unmanaged, it can control you. To avoid detonating an atomic bomb, you need to learn how to harness anger's power.

If you do not handle anger carefully and thoughtfully, it can take over your life. Attempting to gain power, you feel powerless in its grasp. A distinguishing mark of addiction is excessiveness. Your anger is too much or too little. AA claims that any addiction affects your body, mind, and emotions. Alcoholism is defined as, "an allergy of the body to alcohol," "a mental obsession," "an insane urge," and "instincts run wild." Similarly, anger affects the whole person, making your life out of balance.

How does anger become so out of balance despite your best efforts to manage it? All or some of the following may be affecting your ability to manage your anger:

- You were born with a brain on high alert to danger.

- Your temperament is prone to excess.

- Your family struggled with aggression.

- Your culture craves power and glory.

The Emotional Brain: Alert to Danger

Our brain is a finely tuned instrument to help us survive, thrive, and grow. Functioning properly, it enables us to keep our balance in a topsy-turvy, challenging, and dangerous world. However, if it's chemical balance is upset, mental illness results.

Science has come to understand how our brains have evolved over millions of years and share common features with our cousins in the animal world (1). The most primitive part of the "old brain" is the brainstem surrounding the top of the spinal cord. This part of the anatomy, sometimes called the "reptilian brain," regulates vital life functions like breathing, the metabolism of the organs, and automatic reactions to the environment. Emerging from this primitive root is the "emotional brain," which regulates our more complex emotional reactions to the world around us. The emotions spur us to action for our survival and wellbeing. They may tell us to approach or avoid an experience that is deemed helpful or harmful. About a million years ago, the brains of mammals had a growth spurt. Layers of complex, interacting cells grew over the emotional brain to form the neo-cortex, or "new brain." This region, most developed in us humans, enables planning, thinking, and coordinating movements. It also helps us to regulate our emotions.

Looking more closely at the emotional brain, one of its essential functions is the detection of danger. We are hardwired to seek safety. Briefly, here is how it works. There is both a fast track and a slow track. When some danger is detected by the senses, a signal is sent through the thalamus almost instantaneously to the amygdala, a small, almond shaped group of neurons. The amygdala acts as a storehouse of emotional memories of what has been harmful or helpful to us. Some of these impressions are from early childhood. The amygdala acts like a prerational emotional watch guard that asks if what is experienced is something to hate, fear, or embrace. If danger is detected, a crisis message is spread immediately throughout the brain. The message triggers the release of hormones, particularly norepinephrine and cortisol, that activate the movement centers. The body is then in a state of emergency to act quickly. It can react in three general ways to the perceived danger: fight, flight, or freeze.

The fast track response evolved to protect us from immediate danger, like an attacking animal or a fast-approaching car. There is no time to think. Spontaneous action is required for safety. However, the quick response may not always be the best response. It can lead to leaping before looking. The danger may be exaggerated, the reaction excessive. The automatic response may not be the most effective in the moment or the long-term. For example, you may swear at someone because you thought he insulted you. The rational brain is hijacked in the face of the perceived danger.

In contrast, the slow track response can help avoid the possible catastrophes of the automatic reaction. Sensory signals of possible danger travel a longer, slower route to the prefrontal lobes behind the forehead. These lobes are part of the neocortex, the "new brain," which is the seat of thinking, planning, and moving toward goals. The prefrontal lobes quickly analyze the incoming data, assess the risk, and consider possible actions. The circuitry in this brain area is more complex, considers many alternatives from the memory store, and takes time to decide how to act. The left frontal lobe, in particular, acts as a neural thermostat to regulate unpleasant emotions. It can switch off or dampen powerful emotions. Furthermore, it decides if the best course of action is to fight, flee, or freeze in the face of the threat.

That all sounds so simple. We only need to stop and think to avoid excessive anger reactions. However, the situation is more complex. The new brain makes decisions based on information that is both conscious and unconscious. It cannot escape the danger of bias from our temperament, our family experience, and our culture.

Temperament: the Inborn Bias

All of us are born with a unique temperament that is hardwired into our genes. In the face of perceived danger, we are predisposed to react with anger in fighting against it, with fear and anxiety to run away from it, or with sadness and depression to freeze in the face of it. We all have tendencies to react in extremes if we do not check ourselves.

Mark, a hothead:

"I've been a fighter my whole life. I was a strong-willed child and threw temper tantrums. My parents told me I was born like I was shot from a gun, active and stubborn. I never liked anyone telling me what to do. Of course, that caused many problems in school. I was sent to the principal's office more times than I can count. Somehow, I got through college and joined the work force. I had trouble with authority and could not follow directions that made no sense to me. After being fired a few times for my big mouth, I decided I had to be my own boss, so I started a business that is now thriving. I have something that's mine that I can put all my energy into."

Some are born with an aggressive temperament, the "choleric" personality. They possess a strong sense of their own power and want things done their way. They are the Frank Sinatras of this world. In the face of any obstacle or danger, they refuse to back down. They possess a high level of energy and willingness to fight for what they want. They despise weakness. Power and control motivate them. Many are the type-A personalities that are driven to perfection and success. These personalities embody the masculine ideal in our society.

Gabriel, a worry-wort:

> *"I was shy as a child and enjoyed playing alone. My parents pushed me to go outside to play with other kids, but I always resisted. I felt safe at home and didn't want to leave. Even now as an adult, I'm a homebody. When I'm with other people, I worry about what they are thinking. I'm self-conscious about my weight and think everyone is looking at me and making fun of me. It was terrible for me in school. I tried to be as invisible as I could because I was so anxious."*

Others are born with an anxious temperament. Their brain is always on high alert. They are surrounded by dangers at every turn and feel helpless to face them. They are the wall flowers in any social group. In the face of any perceived danger, they want to run away. They may physically remove themselves from situations where they feel threatened. They may withdraw into their minds and worry. The pursuit of safety and security motivates them. Rituals, routines, and rules give them a sense of safety in a dangerous world.

Kelly, helplessly dependent:

> *"I married my husband because I admired his strength. I knew he would take care of me. He was a man who took charge of things, and I could rely on him. When he died, my life fell apart. I didn't know what to do. My children could see how lost I was and supported me through my grief. Now, there is another problem. It's about money. My children are telling me I have to sell some things and invest in other things. I don't know what to do. What's worse is that the children don't agree on a plan and are fighting with each other. Some are telling me to do one thing, while others are telling me to do the opposite. I can't stand anyone being angry with me, so I do nothing. I'm so depressed."*

Still others have a melancholic temperament. They are predisposed to focus on what is missing in their lives, bemoan the losses, and feel helpless to move forward. In the face of any confrontation, they feel threatened. They freeze and do not know what they want or what to do. They fear asserting themselves because someone may not like them. Approval and a sense of belonging motivate them. They cling to others from whom they imagine drawing their strength. They only see weakness in themselves. Many assume the self-sacrificing female role that was once prized in our culture.

Family Legacy: The Homegrown Bias

While our temperament provides one bias in assessing danger and how to respond, the messages about anger from our childhoods present another bias. Anger is a family affair. Each of us has a unique history that shapes our thinking, feeling, and behaving. We receive messages from our parents about life and relationships that influence our views of ourselves and the world.

Whenever I meet with a patient struggling with anger, I always ask them to explore the family roots of their reactions. For example, I asked Melinda, who struggled with her temper, "Where did you learn to express your anger that way?"

Melinda responded, "It seems like I had a temper my whole life. When I think about it, I'm not surprised. My father had a terrible temper, and we were afraid of him. He wasn't violent, but his yelling terrified us. The smallest thing set him off. Despite all my efforts, I became just like him. He could not control himself, so I never learned how to control myself."

"How about your mother?" I asked.

"Well, she was a quiet woman who never spoke up. I think she was terrified of my father, like all of us. I knew I didn't want to be like her, so submissive. That wasn't in my nature. I guess what I saw was two extremes in my parents. My father had little control, and my mother seemed to swallow her anger or not have any at all. I've never learned the middle ground," Melinda reflected. After a pause, she added, "I married a man who is more like my mother. He's so laid back. He just goes along with whatever I want. Sometimes I wish he would speak up more."

"What about the rest of your family?" I asked.

"My father's side was a bunch of hot-headed Italians. They were loud and argued constantly. They also had tempers. However, after any explosion, it was over. My mother's side was German. They held their feelings in and didn't talk much, but they could be stubborn. One thing I'm glad about is that neither side drinks much. My closest friend is from an Irish family. They are the nicest, friendliest people you'd ever want to meet, but when they drink, all hell breaks loose."

Our parents are role models on how to manage our emotions, especially the intense feeling of anger. As children, we were sponges soaking up their influences. We may not be aware of the power of their messages until we take the time to stop and think about what has shaped our lives. "The past is not dead, it is not even past," William Faulkner observed. Our past lives through us. As we become more aware of its messages, we can learn to disengage, evaluate, and choose to act differently.

A further powerful influence on how we work with our anger comes from extreme expressions of it when growing up. At one extreme, we may have been abused verbally and/or physically by our parents. We may have witnessed fighting and violence. At the other extreme, we may have experienced emotional neglect by our parents. Perhaps they were self-absorbed in work or addictions, and we felt alone. Such experiences profoundly affect the way you regulate your own emotions.

Two common patterns of emotional regulation are common. You may identify with the aggressor and struggle to contain your own anger. You become fascinated with its power and emulate your aggressive parent. Or you may identify with the victim and learn to suppress the natural energy of your anger. You fear the harm you may cause if you let yourself feel its power.

America's Pursuit of Power and Glory: The Cultural Bias

We receive a third group of messages about anger from our culture. Every culture presents rules about the appropriate expression and use of anger. Some of these rules are explicit, while others are not. Its influence is like the air we breathe. We cannot live without it, yet we take it for granted. We may not notice the impurities in the air until it causes problems. Only anger gone awry wakes us up to the bias.

The recent election of Donald Trump (2016) highlighted our biases. His win surprised and shocked our country and the world. Half the country loved him, while the other half hated him. Few were neutral. Throughout the campaign he was the underdog and the Washington outsider fighting to bring change. His campaign slogan was, "Make America Great Again." That message resonated with enough voters to get him elected. I asked some of my friends and relatives what that slogan meant to them. Here are some responses:

> *"The United States is no longer a powerhouse. We are seen as weak around the world. We've lost respect. Other nations take advantage of us economically. Our trade agreements are unfair. Immigrants cross our borders at will and take away jobs. Terrorists have no fear of us."*

> *"We have become a weak nation and have to be strong again. We have to make our borders safer. We have to destroy ISIS and not fool around with them. We have to have a stronger military. We have to have a better economy and keep jobs at home. We have to be tougher on crime."*

> *"It's all about wealth, patriotism, and morality. We've lost our greatness because we've compromised our old-fashioned values. Our economy has suffered because jobs have left and outsiders have come in. We're not self-sufficient anymore. People don't take pride in our country anymore. We've compromised our values allowing abortions and gay marriages."*

Trump's message resonated with the current electorate and touched on core values within our American culture. These core values, which have made America unique and great, also foster a particular attitude toward the expression and use of the energy of anger. America has always been dedicated to the pursuit of glory and power. Its bias is more toward the release than the restraint of anger. We are more active than passive in pursuing our goals. We are more optimistic than pessimistic about change and progress, which require the judicious use of anger's energy. Let's look at some of our core values and how they promote the expression, and possible excessive use, of anger.

Rugged Individualism: Our Puritan ancestors did not fit in with the pack. They were outsiders, persecuted for their religious beliefs. They wanted to pursue pure, undiluted Gospel values, and were not content with mediocrity. They wanted to be the best, all that God wanted them to be. They exhibited a rebellious spirit in criticizing the religious practice of the day. However, persecution did not defeat them. It toughened them. Courageously, they left the security of their homeland to settle in a brave new world.

The desire to be a separate individual can foster a "we-against-them mentality" that fuels the release of anger. Others can be seen as competitors for limited resources, or even enemies. Only one can be the best. Others need to be defeated for us to be number one. "The survival of the fittest" can easily become our motto, leading to a fighting spirit.

Practical Action: "I'm from Missouri, show me." We want to see results, not just hear words. Idle speculation bores us. We are a success-driven people. We believe in the Protestant work ethic. Success is not from chance or fate. It is earned through hard work. We believe that, in working, we share in the creative power of God. He made us responsible to care for the earth and have dominion over all the living creatures on the earth.

Pragmatism invites us to take an active, not a passive, stance toward life. In the face of obstacles, our mandate is to overcome them, to fight for what we want. In the face of danger, we stand our ground, instead of running away in fear or withdrawing into depression. Anger is an energy for change. Our task is to use that energy wisely for benefit, not harm.

Moral Idealism: As a child, class began for us each day with a recitation of the Pledge of Allegiance: "I pledge allegiance to the flag of the United States of America and to the republic for which it stands, one nation, under God, indivisible, with liberty and justice for all." That is a noble vow to make each day. It expresses the high standards upon which our country was founded. Our Puritan ancestors fled religious persecution and dedicated themselves to ensuring liberty and justice for all. It was their way of glorifying God. Following in their footsteps, we attempt to free ourselves as well as others. We have become missionaries of democracy and defenders of human rights around the world, fearlessly fighting wars to protect the freedom of nations.

"The road to disappointment and resentment is paved by expectation," the AA saying warns. If idealism becomes excessive, it can foster conflict and turmoil. Our idealism has promoted liberation movements for racial minorities, women, gays, the disabled, the poor, and so forth. The gap between our expectations and reality invites hard work to close it. That anger, of course, can become excessive, leading to violence, but it can also be energy for needed change.

Pioneering Spirit: I grew up watching the Lone Ranger and John Wayne movies. They embodied the toughness, courage, and adventure of the American spirit. Our ancestors were not settlers. They believed in progress, in moving ahead despite all obstacles. They were also open to new frontiers and new adventures. Instead of clinging to the past and worn-out traditions, they embarked on a journey that expanded their horizons. They undertook an errand into the wilderness to create a new life in a Promised Land.

Progress requires movement; movement requires a willingness to change; and change needs energy. The law of inertia is powerful. It can only be overcome by a stronger energy. That energy is the hope anger can give for positive change. We are not inclined, as Americans, to succumb to the deadening inertia of fear or depression. As Roosevelt urged in leading us to battle in World War II, "There is nothing to fear but fear itself."

These core values translate into messages. We often hear two competing messages about anger: "Don't rock the boat," and, "The squeaky wheel gets the grease." Our current cultural messages, however, emphasize more the release than restraint of anger. It appears that the messages of restraint from our Puritan ancestors, such as, "Turn the other cheek," "See anger as a temptation from the devil," and, "Practice self-control," have been pushed into the background. The following are some more common messages today:

- "Stand up for yourself and be counted."
- "Don't let people push you around."

- "Compete, fight to be the best."

- "Aim high. Don't settle."

- "Be free to express yourself."

- "Be strong and don't show any weakness."

- "Fight for what you believe in."

The core American values inspire the release of the energy of anger. Whether that energy is used for benefit or harm depends on the depth of our wisdom and compassion.

In response to a perceived threat, our brain provides a selection of responses: fight, flight, or freeze. The inclination of our temperament, the sway of our family experience, and the messages from our culture, influence how, when, and where we express anger's vital energy.

4

The Addictive Personality:
Self-Will Run Riot

*"The intoxication of anger, like that of the grape,
shows us to others, but hides us from ourselves."*

—Charles Caleb Colton

I took pride in my self-control. I was hardworking and conscientious, and I never displayed any temper. Others noticed my exterior peace and asked, "How do you stay so calm? Don't you ever get angry? Still waters must run deep." They seemed to admire my apparent tranquility, and I enjoyed their admiration. What others did not know, and what I did not admit to myself, was the fear inside. I was like a duck floating leisurely while paddling madly to keep moving. I suffered from an anxious temper. It was fear that made me avoid any confrontation. I subtly manipulated others, telling them what they wanted to hear, to keep them from getting angry with me. What appeared to be so self-sacrificing was an illusion that disguised a self-centered fear.

AA describes the heart of addiction as "self-centered fear." Addictions begin with a sense of helplessness, of fear, living in a threatening world. To compensate for their sense of powerlessness, alcoholics discover in alcohol a magical power. Alcohol makes their problems disappear. As they continue drinking, they become more dependent on this outside agent, their drug of choice, to feel good. Their thinking, emotional responses, and behaviors follow a predictable pattern, making them more fearful of being overwhelmed. These progressively engrained reactions become habitual, shaping the personality and character. The final outcome, the destiny, accurately expressed by Alcoholics Anonymous, is "insanity and death."

In a similar way, those who suffer an anger sickness experience a self-centered fear. They view the world as a threatening place and see enemies everywhere, especially in themselves. As the saying goes, "When I look in the mirror, I see the enemy. It is me."

Naturally, they seek ways to defend themselves to feel safe. In their anger, they find that power, like a drug that offers the promise of power, control, and safety. However, the more they express their anger in hostile thoughts, words, and actions, the more unbalanced their lives become, tilted toward the negative. They direct their attacks against both others and themselves. Over time, their habitual reactions shape their character and destiny. They see themselves as "an angry person." The well-known slogan reveals their destiny, "He who lives by the sword, dies by the sword." Their aggression leads to "insanity and death."

Whenever anger is lived in the extremes, whether overly indulged or suppressed, your personality becomes unbalanced. You may exhibit these personality traits:

- You feel powerless and become preoccupied with gaining power and control.

- You feel threatened and protect yourself with blaming.

- Your excessive and misdirected anger causes both pleasure and pain.

- You see enemies everywhere and brood about being wronged and treated unfairly.

- You become childlike in your sense of helplessness.

Power Hungry, Power Starved

Alcoholics Anonymous describes alcoholism as "self-will run riot." The Steps/Traditions Book adds: "Our whole trouble had been the misuse of willpower. We had tried to bombard our problems with it..."(1). Alcoholics want power and control over their lives. When they run into problems, they use their mind and mood altering drug to make the world go away. If they experience some uncomfortable feeling, like sadness, anger, or anxiety, they can make those emotions disappear in an intoxicated fog.

As the alcoholic indulges his fantasy of control with the bottle, however, the addiction begins to tighten its grip on his life. Believing he is exerting power over his life by drinking, alcohol becomes his master and enslaves him. Gradually, he loses his ability to choose to drink. He drinks because he needs to in order to avoid painful withdrawal symptoms and to feel normal. As the illness progresses, he tragically loses his life. The well-known adage expresses this progression: "First, the man takes the drink; then, the drink takes the drink; then, the drink takes the man."

Like the addict, you may feel out of control with your anger. Initially, it made you feel powerful, especially if you felt helpless in some area of your life. You could influence situations and get your way. You believe others respect you for standing up for yourself. However, if your anger becomes excessive, people back away from you. They may see you as a bully. You sense their withdrawal and may feel guilt for your temper outbursts. Anger has become your master; you are its slave.

Catherine, ruled by anger:

"My father was a violent man, and all of us were afraid of him. Nevertheless, I always tried to please him, gain his approval. I felt like I never succeeded, so I devoted myself to being the best in school. I was intelligent, worked hard, and did very well. My goal was to be an attorney and help abused women. After passing the bar exam, I worked in a law firm specializing in divorce cases. My case load was mostly of women who were battered. I fought hard for them. Some say I was a ferocious advocate. I felt like I was making a difference. There was a rage in me. Unfortunately, I took my anger home. Without realizing it, I became demanding and impatient with my husband and children. I had temper outbursts. The children cowered, and my husband complained. One day I woke up and realized I had become my father, and I felt a terrible guilt."

The natural energy of anger can be a powerful force for good when used well. It is a gift. You stand up for yourself and develop healthy self-esteem. You may have an exquisite sense of justice and courageously fight for the wellbeing of others. However, anger can become intoxicating. The adrenaline rush and power over others can seduce you. You love getting your way. Without knowing it, you may cross an invisible line and become possessed by the anger. You become a bully, aggressive with others, disrespectful of their sensitivities. People fear you. They either fight back or withdraw from you. Instead of feeling pride in your strength, you begin to feel shame and guilt. The injustice you protested you now inflict on others.

Unlike an addiction to alcohol or drugs, you can have too little anger. You can live a full life without drinking, but not without the energy of anger. If you are frightened by the power of anger because of your temperament or what you witnessed growing up, you may bottle it up. However, the buried anger, like lava, does not stay dormant. It may burn up your insides, making you physically sick, depressed, and anxious. It may also erupt occasionally or seep out through the cracks in your self-control.

Alice, a self-proclaimed wimp:

"My mother was a kind, gentle woman. She sacrificed herself for the family and never asked anything for herself. She took such good care of us and never thought about herself. I admired those qualities. I became an obedient child. As an adult, I worked hard at my office job. I would do anything anyone asked and enjoyed helping others. Whenever something extra needed to be done, my coworkers assumed, 'Alice will do it.' I never hesitated to do the extra work and even took work home. At some point, I felt burned out and could hardly get out of bed in the morning. I used to look forward to my job, but now I dreaded it. I wasn't sure why. I had the feeling that people were taking advantage of me, and I didn't speak up. I felt like such a wimp. I guess I was getting depressed."

Anger is a life-giving energy. It can motivate you to overcome inertia and take action, to assert yourself. Using it to help others enhances your own and others' wellbeing. However, if you do not use that energy on your own behalf to protect yourself and set boundaries, you can make yourself defenseless. You allow others to intrude in your personal space. The result is that you make yourself powerless in your world. You can then become depressed and fearful. Another name for depression is "learned helplessness." By suppressing your anger, you teach yourself to be helpless. Anxiety arises when you feel unable to protect yourself. By denying your own natural power, you disable yourself.

Both the alcoholic and the anger addicted have a distorted relationship to power. The alcoholic exerts his will power to control his mind and moods, disengaging from reality. Suffering an anger sickness, you may either over-control or under-control its expression. If you lose a balanced relationship with it, you will become anger's slave. Anger can be a harsh master, making you ashamed, depressed, or fearful.

Hostile Self-Centeredness

You may be surprised to hear that at the heart of any addiction is self-centeredness, and not the drinking or drug use. The Alcoholics Anonymous Big Book (2) states: "Self-ishness—self-centeredness! That, we think, is the root of our troubles." Drinking to get intoxicated is a selfish act. No one or nothing else matters when an alcoholic is in the midst of a binge. All cares, worries, and responsibilities are cast aside. All the pleading of family, friends, and concerned others meets deaf ears. As the addiction progresses, the alcoholic becomes more self-centered, living only for the party. Consuming alcohol becomes the organizing principle of his life, leaving little room for anyone or anything else.

The consequences of progressive alcoholic drinking inevitably lead to isolation. The Steps/Traditions Book states: "Almost without exception, alcoholics are tortured by lone-liness. Even before our drinking got bad and people began cutting us off, nearly all of us suffered the feeling that we didn't quite belong"(p. 57). The self-centered, exclusive con-sumption of alcohol drives others away and reduces the alcoholic's social world to himself, his drinking buddies, and his bottle. The drinking leads to a lonely existence, which in turn becomes the excuse for more drinking. In the process, the alcoholic comes to hate himself, but feels powerless to stop the insane cycle.

The bottle-induced loneliness also results in feelings of emotional insecurity. The alco-holic tries desperately to connect with people to relieve his painful isolation. Unwittingly, he connects in immature and self-defeating ways. "Either we had tried to play God and dominate those about us, or we had insisted on being dependent on them" (p. 115), the Steps/Traditions Book observes. Driven by insecurity, he either tries to dominate others, making himself feel powerful, or he becomes dependent on them, indulging his sense of helplessness.

Like the alcoholic, you neglect to take realistic responsibility for yourself. You play the blame game. Secretly, you believe that the world revolves around you, as if you were God. The blame, of course, moves in two directions—towards others and yourself. When others do not meet your expectations, you become disappointed and blame them. Your misery is their entire fault. You are not the cause of your own troubles. In retaliation, you may criticize, correct, and try to dominate them. You argue and blame, convinced you are right. Your relationships become contentious. You end up alone and isolated.

Brook, an adolescent blaming her mother:

"I hate my mother. She constantly criticized me for being too heavy. I became so self-conscious about my weight. I tried to diet and took it too far. I starved myself. Mom and I argued all the time about every little thing. She wanted to tell me what to do about my diet, school work, and my friends. I resented her sticking her nose in my business. After our arguments, I went into the bathroom and cut myself. I want to stay as far away from her as I can. I don't care if I ever see my mother again."

In contrast, you may direct the blame for anything that goes wrong in your life and around you on yourself. "I'm the sole cause of all the misery; it's all my fault," you tell yourself. Of course, you never take credit for anything going right. Instead of judging others, you judge yourself by high standards, which you can never reach. A sense of failure dominates your life. You also feel helpless to correct problems or improve yourself. Others may try to console you, but eventually become tired of your insistent self-deprecation. You end up isolating yourself, stewing in the soup of your self-blame.

Louise, blaming herself:

"I was married to an alcoholic for many years, but didn't even know it. He got drunk regularly, but I thought that was normal. When he drank, he had a temper and said terrible things to me and the kids. I finally woke up when I saw how afraid the kids were of him and filed for divorce. He never wanted the divorce and kept telling me I was making a big mistake. He told me I was being selfish, and that I kept the children away from him and was hurting them. I began doubting myself and thought about calling off the divorce. I was worried about him and thought I was the one causing all the problems."

Both the alcoholic and the anger obsessed become self-absorbed in their illnesses. They think of themselves as the center of the universe and lose perspective on life. The alcoholic withdraws into the bottle, ignores responsibilities, and alienates others. Those with an anger sickness avoid a realistic sense of personal responsibility, either by blaming others or themselves excessively. It is only finding a balance in responsible care, both for themselves and others, that leads to growth.

A Murderously Sweet Emotion

Alcoholics seek pleasure and avoid pain, at all costs. The Steps/Traditions Book observes: "Instinct run wild in themselves is the underlying cause of their destructive drinking"(p. 44). Alcoholics, in their self-centeredness, want to indulge their needs. They want immediate gratification, without limits. They want it all and want it now. They dive headlong into the chase.

While chasing the high, alcoholics are also running away from pain. Most alcoholics, in my experience, are sensitive people who are overwhelmed by life. They seek to medicate intolerable pain through their drug, alcohol. The Steps/Traditions Book comments: "Our lives have been largely devoted to running away from pain and problems. We fled from them as from a plague. We never wanted to deal with the fact of suffering. Escape via the bottle was our solution"(p. 74). However, the solution becomes the problem over time.

Running away from pain and problems through drinking becomes a way of life. The pain and problems do not disappear when ignored. They grow in intensity and cause more suffering, which becomes another excuse to drink more.

Caught up in anger, you also become preoccupied with seeking pleasure and avoiding pain. Anger becomes your drug, a stimulant that both energizes and numbs you. It also enables you to avoid full responsibility for your life.

Peter, dreaming of revenge:

"I was shocked when my wife served me divorce papers. We had our problems, but I never expected her to walk out of the marriage. I begged and pleaded with her to stay, but she had her mind made up. After she left, I went into a tailspin. I became depressed and drank a lot. I thought my life was over and even thought about suicide. Then one day, something shifted inside me. I became enraged at what she had done and how she had wronged me. The anger grew and I thought about ways of getting back at her. Now I read the obituaries every day hoping to see her name. Since I never see her, my revenge will be outliving her."

Indulged anger serves a dual purpose. First, it gives you a sense of power, especially when you are feeling powerless. You become energized with a new focus on life. In an angry state of mind, you identify an enemy, the one who harmed you. You have a purpose. Your mind makes plans on how you can get revenge. That revenge is sweet. You imagine that it will take away all the pain of the offense.

Anger also medicates the pain of loss. When you have lost something important to you, you naturally feel sadness and even anxiety about more losses to come. The anger shifts your mood from a sense of helplessness to power. Your anger can disguise sadness and fear, whose roots may go back to childhood. One patient of mine told me her mother had committed suicide when she was five years old. She said, "I've never gotten over the loss. I'm enraged about it and have temper outbursts. I know it's grief behind my temper, but I can't help myself. I'm afraid the sorrow would swallow me up if I didn't stay angry." An irritable mood may also disguise guilt. Another patient told me, "I had a one night stand while drunk one night. My wife never knew. I felt terribly guilty. I got an attitude and picked fights with my wife. I guess I wanted her to punish me."

Like any drug, the anger provides temporary relief. The angel of mercy soon betrays you and becomes a demon of misery. The first and perhaps greatest psychologist, who lived twenty six hundred years ago, was the Buddha. Many today are learning to appreciate his wisdom, which he expressed in clear, common sense language. He observed, "Holding on to anger is like grasping a hot coal with the intent of throwing it at someone else; you are the one who gets burned."

Negative Thinking

Alcoholics suffer from distorted thinking that takes them on a path to destruction. They are "victims of a mental obsession," and, "smitten by an insane urge," the Steps/Traditions book notes (p. 22). They believe they can find happiness and escape the vicissitudes of life with alcohol. As the addiction deepens, their lives become more and more organized around the pursuit of alcohol and "chasing the high." They rationalize to themselves and others countless reasons for drinking. They tell themselves they cannot resist the urge. They claim they need to drink because they are sad, happy, angry, stressed out. In reality, alcoholics drink because they are addicted.

"Stinking thinking," as it does for the alcoholic, fuels the anger impulse. You complain, "Life is so unfair. I always get the short end of the stick. Everybody is against me." You see those who have harmed you as your enemies and presume malevolent intentions on their part. The wound festers. Thoughts of sweet revenge fill your mind, and the anger grows. You want the offender to feel your pain, so you plot ways of retaliating. "An eye for an eye, and a tooth for a tooth," the Bible says. "I only want justice," you tell yourself. Your thinking becomes more distorted, running on a negative track as the hostile feelings possess you. A German proverb states, "Fire in the heart sends smoke to the head."

The enemy in your mind does not need to be a person. It can be a situation in your life that you judge unfair. You may even consider life itself unfair and believe you are a victim of fate. Where, then, can you direct your anger? Against whom can you seek revenge? Against God? In your irrational state of mind, you will probably direct your hostility against yourself.

Matthew, complaining of life's unfairness:

"I was diagnosed with bipolar disorder as a teenager. That was totally unfair to be born with a mental illness. I was prescribed medications, but I hated taking them. I just wanted to be normal. When I was feeling good for a while, I believed I was finally cured, so I decided to stop taking them. A few days later I was overwhelmed with a feeling of sadness I could hardly stand. I was irritable and snapped at everyone. I hated what I was doing, but couldn't stop myself. I lost interest in everything and just wanted to sleep. I hated myself and just wanted to die. I was too embarrassed to tell anyone about how bad I felt. Fortunately, my parents confronted me and got me help again. I still long for the day I will be cured, so I can be like everybody else."

High expectations fuel anger and all addictions. "The road to disappointment and resentment is paved by expectation," AA warns. You have the gnawing feeling that your life is not enough. You want more, so you work harder for more money, success, power, love. Yet nothing seems to fill the void. You complain and look for someone or something to blame for your unhappiness. Yet the answer eludes you. You feel like the man who lost his key in the dark and looks under the street light even though he knows he did not lose it there. Instead, look within yourself. Look at your expectations about yourself and your life. Most often, perfectionism and unrealistic expectations feed your anger.

Kenneth, a dissatisfied perfectionist:

"My favorite word is 'but.' Whenever anyone tells me something good, I always qualify it. Nothing can be good enough. I'm always judging myself and people. I know this is a strange way to think, but I can't help myself. I used to love to go to church, but I don't anymore. Why? Because I think everyone there is a hypocrite. I notice how they dress inappropriately, come late, and talk during services. I hate to

invite people into my home because it is never clean enough. I wonder what people are thinking and imagine they are judging me."

Both alcoholics and those consumed by anger have a one track mind toward the negative. The glass is always half full or broken. Alcoholics think they need a drink to cope with life's troubles. Preoccupation with being wronged and the unfairness of life justifies their outrage. Life is not the way they wish it would be, and they believe their anger will make them feel better.

Stuck in Childhood

The Steps/Traditions Book reported a study by psychologists and doctors of a group of problem drinkers in the early years of AA. Their conclusions shocked the AA members at the time. The researchers concluded that, "most of the alcoholics under investigation were still childish, emotionally sensitive, and grandiose"(p. 123).

After an initial protest, the AA membership, over time, has come to acknowledge the accuracy of the observations of those early researchers. Those in recovery learned how much their personalities were formed by their years of drinking to make them childlike and irresponsible. Driven by unreasonable fears and anxieties, they developed a false pride to compensate for their deep emotional insecurities. Like children, they became self-centered in the extreme, seeking the immediate gratification of their desires. They ignored responsibilities to family, friends, and work, seeking only to escape pain and problems in the bottle. They avoided anything unpleasant and indulged their fantasy to create a carefree life through drinking. In short, the alcoholic regressed to become a child again in his obsessive pursuit of pleasure and avoidance of personal responsibility.

Like the alcoholic, when you are hooked on anger, you regress to become like a child again. Watch how children play with each other. You notice that some children bend the rules to suit them while playing games. They are impatient for their turn and cannot tolerate losing. When they do not get their way, they throw temper tantrums. Other children sit on the sidelines. They do not become involved unless someone leads them. They are afraid to assert themselves. Still others engage freely in the give-and-take of the game. They enjoy themselves, try hard, and accept the consequences. How children play the game reveals their level of maturity. When you suffer an anger sickness, you may throw temper tantrums or refuse to become actively involved in life.

Meredith, a stubborn woman with a temper:

"I'm a stubborn person. I both love and hate that quality in me. If I believe I'm right, I'm willing to fight hard for my opinion and won't back down. People accuse me of being closed-minded and thinking I'm always right. I'm just opinionated and thoughtful about my point of view. There's a fine line between having an open mind and a hole in your head. What I don't like about my stubbornness is that I can quickly come to a boil if people oppose me too much. I can fly into a rage. Then I feel like a two year old having a temper tantrum."

James, sitting on the sidelines of life:

> *"I've always been a shy and anxious person. I was so self-conscious when I was around people that I avoided going out. As a teenager, I discovered marijuana as a way to chill out. My parents pushed me pretty hard in school because I did the minimal work and barely passed. I've been in college for five years now and have no idea what I want to do with my life. I'm just taking classes to have something to do. I feel so lost."*

The challenge for both alcoholics and the anger addicted is to grow up. Both are stuck in childhood, with the "infantile omnipotence" ways of thinking and behaving. They believe the world revolves around them and should serve their needs. They have difficulty tolerating any frustration and can be demanding. They entertain high expectations of themselves and others. When they do not get their way, they may throw temper tantrums, withdraw, or drink. Focused on seeking pleasure and avoiding pain at all costs, they ignore their adult responsibilities.

Despite feeling trapped in your anger illness, there is a cure that awaits you. Even though your anger may numb and possess you, you can loosen its grip on you. You can come to know yourself and mature in your thinking and behaving. However, it will require hard work and a willingness to surrender your illusions about life.

PART TWO:
FREEDOM THROUGH FORGIVENESS

Dennis Ortman, Ph.D.

The Steps: Toward Freedom and Forgiveness

"Progress is impossible without change, and those who cannot change their minds cannot change anything."

—George Bernard Shaw

"If there is a healing to be done, that healing would be to wake up. This is the greatest healing."

—Mooji

When I walked into the room, my nerves almost got the best of me. I was not sure I was doing the right thing or was in the right place. The group of women sitting at the table looked up at me, smiled, and said, "Welcome." They introduced themselves and invited me to take a seat. After a brief introduction by the leader, each of the women in turn talked about their struggle coping with the drinking of their family member. They spoke about being hurt and coming to forgiveness. There was no blame. They spoke honestly, expressed hope, and offered each other support. As the discussion continued, I felt myself relax. I knew I had come to the right place. It was an Al-Anon meeting. I came because I was so angry at my family's drinking.

Al-Anon follows the Twelve Step program of Alcoholics Anonymous. Originally, alcoholics found that the steps proved an effective path for recovery from their addiction. Their family members discovered that they suffered from a disease called "codependency," and working the steps gave them relief. Over the years, the Twelve Step program has helped those with a variety of behaviors recognized as addictive, such as overeating, over-sexing, gambling, compulsive shopping, and so forth. Twelve Step groups addressing these problems sprung up all over the world. Now groups have emerged, such as Emotions Anonymous, acknowledging that we can become addicted to mood states and self-defeating habits of thinking.

How did this powerful program of healing and growth begin?

Bill Wilson's Spiritual Awakening

The roots of AA (1) extend back to the days of the Depression, the 1930s. The place was the Midwest, Akron, Ohio. Bill Wilson, the founder, was a hopeless drunk and severely depressed. His drinking binges cost him his job, strain on his marriage, and his emotional health. He was hospitalized numerous times, but continued to relapse. The dark cloud of despair enshrouded him.

Then one day, an old drinking buddy called to visit. When he arrived, Bill offered him a drink, which he refused. Bill was shocked and asked him the reason. His friend simply responded, "I've got religion." He told Bill how a simple religious idea changed his life and brought him to sobriety. Bill, who thought of himself as an intelligent rationalist, was skeptical. He was not an atheist, but resisted the thought of a personal God, a Czar of the Heavens. His friend suggested, "Why don't you choose your own conception of God?" That idea hit home. It was possible to separate your personal experience of God from all the different ideas about Him taught by the churches. A seed was planted.

Bill was involved in a Christian fellowship called the Oxford Group. This organization taught that the root of all our problems is in fear and selfishness. The antidote was to pursue universal human values in our daily living. The group espoused such practices as making an honest self-examination, acknowledging character defects, making restitution for wrongs, helping others, and surrendering to God. These moral ideas made sense to Bill. He involved himself in trying to help other alcoholics, even though he struggled to remain sober. Despite his dedication to the program, however, he continued to relapse. Nevertheless, with these practices, the seed was being watered.

During what turned out to be his last hospital stay, Bill was at the brink of total despair. He cried out for help to a God he did not believe in. Suddenly, he saw a bright light and felt a peace he never experienced before. He knew then he would never drink again. Bill described the experience as a "hot flash" spiritual conversion. The day that he and his friend Dr. Bob Smith became sober was the birthday of Alcoholics Anonymous. The date was June 6, 1935. A colorful rose bloomed in the darkness of the nation's and Bill's Depression.

Bill then set out to record his experience and the steps that he believed could help others to recover. He began with six steps that closely followed the practices of the Oxford Group. He added detail and expanded the steps to twelve, like the twelve apostles. The heart of the program was the spiritual experience of surrender to God. He said, "The great fact is just this, and nothing else. That we have had deep and effective spiritual experiences which have revolutionized our whole attitude toward life, toward our fellows and toward God's universe" (p. 25). The Alcoholics Anonymous Big Book was first published in 1939.

Following the lead of their founder, devoted members of AA insist that a spiritual conversion of surrender to a Power greater than oneself is crucial to recovery from any addiction. Research has validated this claim. For example, a group of scientists at the Alcohol Research Group in California (2) interviewed alcoholics to determine if there was any correlation between religious belief and how long people stayed sober. They learned that alcoholics who practiced techniques of habit replacement could often stay sober until some stressful event occurred in their lives. Then, they tended to relapse. However, those who had a belief in a Higher Power tended to remain sober even during stressful times.

The Twelve Step program has been so successful for a variety of addictions, especially in our country, because it is a distinctively American program for healing and growth. It addresses head on the many addictive behaviors promoted by our culture of excess.

An American Program of Healing and Growth

What is so uniquely American, and universal, about the Twelve Step program? It embodies several values we hold in high esteem.

Rugged Individualism: Ours is the "land of the free and home of the brave." We believe in the dignity and freedom of every individual and the value of personal responsibility. All are created equal. Each person must trust his own experience and bravely pursue his own destiny in life.

Those addicted to drugs or anger tend to flee from personal responsibility. They blame others for their misery and use it as an excuse for their addictive behaviors. They develop a victim mentality of helplessness. In contrast, the Twelve Steps encourage you to take full responsibility for your life, acknowledge your dignity, and pursue your goals in life. In the process, you are encouraged to trust your own experience.

The AA program also balances the potential one-sidedness of individualism. It encourages belonging to a fellowship for support and strength. "United we stand, divided we fall," the aphorism states. Embedded within our rugged individualism is a desire to belong and work together. The Lone Ranger had Tonto. Batman had Robin. Johnny Carson had Ed McMahon. We also believe that we are stronger together than alone. Because we are united, we help ourselves in helping others.

Moral Idealism: We sometimes forget our spiritual and religious roots. Our founders were devoted Christians. They were persecuted because they took their faith seriously. They wanted freedom to practice their beliefs and live their high moral standards. In coming to the new world, the Puritans believed they were on a missionary errand. They proclaimed liberty and justice for all, particularly religious freedom. Even our coins testify to our faith, "In God we trust."

The heart of addiction is self-centeredness. It is also the excessive pursuit of comfort, power, and control. The steps call for a spiritual awakening and surrender to God's will rather than your own. Instead of a life controlled by self-centered reacting, they promote a value-directed life. The promise is that by working the steps you can achieve freedom from the bondage to your anger and live with forgiveness, the highest form of love. If you direct your anger inward, you can learn to give yourself a break. If you feel vengeful toward those who harmed you, you can forgive them.

Practical Action: We believe in the Protestant work ethic. We believe that hard work will make us successful. We are not helpless victims of fate. Instead, we have a fighting spirit that motivates us to take action. We believe that appropriate action will produce results. Whenever we work to solve a problem, we ask first, "Does it work?" We want to see results.

Those caught up in addictions become lazy. They follow their impulses, chasing pleasure and avoiding pain. They fantasize about the easy life and quick fixes. In contrast, the

AA program insists, "You must work the program; don't expect perfection, just progress." The steps offer practical guidance for leading a good life, but effort is required.

One patient of mine complained, "I didn't know it would be so hard to overcome my anger."

"What made you think it should be easy?" I responded.

The program also promises that if you work the program diligently you will see results. The testimony of millions of members validates that claim.

Pioneering Spirit: We are not, by nature, settlers. By world standards we are a young country and value youth, believing we have everything to look forward to. We look to the future, not the past. We seek the new, not the old. Furthermore, we believe in progress and willingly undertake challenges to improve our lives. We are open to adventure in exploring new frontiers. There is a seeker, an explorer, a cowboy in all of us.

Those who are addicted are stuck. They seek security in fixed thinking, routines, and rituals. Habits rule their lives. They have a merry-go-round existence. In contrast, the steps challenge you to make an inward journey to explore new frontiers in your mind and try new behaviors. You are required to give up old habits and create new ones. That means breaking bad habits and making good ones, replacing anger with compassion.

Confronting the Myth of Control

American values also predispose us to addictions. The myth of control dominates both American thinking and the addictive mind. We aspire to greatness. What does greatness mean for most of us? It means we have power and control over our lives. We are free to choose our destiny and pursue our goals. We can choose where to live, what career to pursue, and what we believe. Opportunity and options are unlimited. Any obstacles we encounter pursuing our goals are challenges that enable us to demonstrate our strength in overcoming them. We aggressively attack those obstacles. Suffering, for us, is loss of control.

Whenever someone comes to me for anger management, I always ask them what they are angry about. They often have a long list of complaints: their job is stressful, their spouse doesn't show enough affection, their neighbor is annoying, and so forth. In some area of their lives they feel powerless and resent it. For example, John complained to me, "I can't stand my job. I've been miserable for a long time. I'm in sales, and every year our sales quota increases. It's ridiculous. What management expects of us is unrealistic. I resent all the pressure I feel from my supervisor."

"What bothers you about the unrealistic sales quotas?" I asked.

"They are unfair. No one can reach them," he responded.

"What do you expect of yourself?" I enquired.

"Success, of course," he said.

"What if you don't reach the goal?" I asked.

"Then there's hell to pay. I'm afraid of being fired. Then I don't know what I'd do," he said.

Behind his anger is fear of failing to meet unrealistic expectations. Behind his fear of failing is dread of losing control of his life. John had to stop and consider what he could or could not control, and then take decisive action.

Bill Wilson observed that alcoholics want to "play God." They want absolute power and control over their lives. Having some control is natural, but the desire becomes an addiction when it is excessive. Then your life becomes out of balance. As in the case of John, fear and anger begin to dominate your life because you feel powerless. Your presumed need for control is not being met. It is difficult to be patient with yourself and others.

The steps offer a balance to an excessive desire for control, which makes you impatient, brittle, and demanding. They pursue the middle path, advising, "Work the program, but let go and let God." They also suggest developing wisdom to understand what you can and cannot control. If you cannot change something, learn to accept it with serenity. If you can, have the courage to take proper action. That means that you cannot control the behavior of those who wrong you. However, you have the power to forgive them from your heart.

The steps further suggest a balance between the masculine and feminine tendencies in our personality. All of us have both male and female elements. On the one hand, the masculine in us tends to be active in pursuing goals, more comfortable in doing tasks. It has a rational, analytic mindset. It also has an aggressive power drive for results. On the other hand, the feminine in us tends to be more open and receptive, embracing life as a whole and accepting mystery. It prefers just being and nurturing relationships. It has an intuitive and affectively sensitive mindset. These qualities exist in varying proportions in each of us. All of us have the task of finding a balance to achieve a sense of wholeness.

Our culture tends to be unbalanced in the excessive pursuit of masculine values, in the desire for action, power, and control. To counteract that tendency, the steps alternate between being passive in contemplating ourselves and being active in pursuing tasks. We are asked to intuit God's will for us and surrender to it. We are also asked to be courageous in making changes in our lives. A Japanese proverb expresses the consequences of an imbalance, "Vision without action is a daydream. Action without vision is a nightmare."

Restoring that balance between action and surrender makes us confront our false assumptions and make a leap of faith.

Four Leaps of Faith

The Steps/Traditions book warns us about the difficulty of this self-confrontation, "All AA's Twelve Steps ask us to go contrary to our natural desires...they all deflate our egos" (p. 55). The steps challenge our ordinary habits of thinking, our conventional perspectives, and our unacknowledged prejudices. They take us to the edge of our comfort zones and ask us to jump into the unknown abyss. It is a leap of faith that promises new life. Working the steps, you have to let yourself be turned upside down, letting your preconceived notions be shattered. I summarize the twelve steps into four leaps of faith:

Dennis Ortman, Ph.D.

FIRST: *"Embrace the discomfort of your anger and learn from it."*

When people come to me for therapy, they say, "I want to get rid of or learn to manage my anger. It has caused so many problems."

After listening to them talk about their struggles with anger and the trouble it causes them, I explain, "I know your anger is painful and you are impatient for relief. You feel powerless over it. Certainly, you cannot stop the natural flow of anger, but you can refrain from acting on it. Your anger is a natural reaction to a perceived threat. It is your friend, not your enemy. Let's take some time to get to know your friend and understand the message it is giving you."

Often, they react with a stunned silence. I have confronted their false assumption that their anger is something negative, their enemy. Instead, I suggest they can learn something from their emotional reaction if they take the risk to embrace it fully. I assure them that the pain can be their teacher if they learn to observe it closely. I suggest the first paradox of recovery: Accepting your pain and powerlessness over your anger, you will be healed.

SECOND: *"Trust in your Higher Power."*

Some of my patients protest, either in words or in their minds, "What does faith have to do with healing my anger sickness? This is a psychological problem, and religion has nothing to do with it. Besides, I came to you because you are a professional psychologist with scientific training. If I wanted spiritual counseling, I would have gone to my priest or minister."

I explain, "You are a whole person, body, mind, and spirit. Your anger affects you at all the levels. There are many different ways to view God, religion, and spirituality. What is important is that you look at your own experience, your hidden longings for something or someone greater in your life. You have a power within that you may not now recognize. It is the power of your conscious awareness. I ask you to trust in your ability to observe yourself and learn."

All of us have a personal religious history. In the secret of our conscience we have asked ourselves ultimate questions about the meaning of life. We have heard the answers of our parents, culture, and various church groups. For many, the conventional answers have not satisfied. Some have suffered so grievously that they cannot believe in a good God. Others have been scandalized by the behavior and narrow-mindedness of many church-goers. This leap of faith invites you to explore more deeply what you really value and what is ultimate for you. Remember that the Divine Reality, however you conceive it, is a Mystery beyond comprehension. This faith leap also asks that you apply that knowledge to your experience of anger. You are God-like in becoming a loving, compassionate, forgiving person. The paradox you face: You surrender to your Higher Power to win.

THIRD: *"Clean house. Your anger is not your problem, only a symptom of the problem."*

Many of my patients take their anger at face value and say, "I'm just angry. That's all there is to it. I realize it is an emotion that has gotten the better of me and that I cannot control. That's the problem as I see it."

I respond, "If the anger is the problem, what keeps you from controlling it? If you say you want to control your temper, just do it. But I know you are here because you have tried many ways to control it and failed. Therapy may be your last resort. Perhaps there is some need buried deep in your anger that is not being met. Your anger may serve a purpose in avoiding that deeper, more frightening problem. If you look closely at your anger, you may discover the hidden benefit for you in hanging on to it."

Most are shocked at my suggestion that there may be a payoff in their anger that makes them reluctant to give it up. While consciously they hate it, they may secretly love it. I invite my patients to unpeel the onion and explore the layers beneath their angry surface. What does your angry reaction reveal about you? What character defect lies beneath the surface of your reacting? What virtue is crying out to be released in your angry reaction? These can be frightening and liberating questions to answer. In seeking the answers, you awaken to the paradox: From weakness comes strength. Facing your anger, you can become a forgiving person.

FOURTH: *"Help yourself by helping others."*

Therapy and self-help groups appear, by definition, to be self-oriented activities. Most come because they have been deeply wounded and have needs that have not been met. They come to be cared for, or, they feel so overwhelmed by their problems that they want someone to give them guidance. Many of my patients tell me, "Please give me some tools to manage my anger. I don't know what to do. I've tried everything and nothing seems to work. You are the expert. I know you have experience in working with people like me and know best what to do."

I respond, "Who is the expert on you?"

"I know I should be, but I'm not," they say.

"What keeps you from knowing what you need for yourself?" I ask.

Those addicted to anger are stuck in childhood without even knowing it. When I point out the childlike thinking that underlies their addictive behaviors, they are often surprised. I explain that recovery is a process of growing up. First, you begin by learning to care for yourself and not depend on others to care for you. You learn what you value and what makes you feel alive. Then you start caring for others, sharing your gifts and developing mutual supportive relationships. As you extend yourself in love to others, you appreciate your own gifts and grow in self-esteem. You live the paradox: We give it away to keep it. Forgiving others benefits you also.

These leaps of faith are supported by the three disciplines suggested by the Serenity Prayer.

The Serenity Prayer: AAA

The attitudes expressed in the famous Serenity Prayer summarize the goal and means of recovery: "Grant me the serenity to accept what I cannot change, the courage to change what I can, and the wisdom to know the difference."

The disciplines needed to work the program toward recovery from your anger addiction are three A's: acceptance, action, and awareness. If you are caught up in an anger addiction, the most difficult attitude to develop is one of acceptance for what you cannot change. Much of your life may feel out of your control. You could not avoid the harm other afflicted on you, the abuse or neglect by your parents, the betrayal of friends, and so forth. To protect yourself, you may entertain the myth of power and control. Your anger is likely a futile effort to compensate for a sense of powerlessness. Revenge, you imagine, will bring justice and peace of mind. However, only a proper attitude of acceptance will give you the serenity, patience, and humility you long for.

Insight can only take you so far. At some point you must decide to take action to improve your life. Those who suppress their anger out of fear or guilt may have difficulty taking appropriate action when it is needed. They may allow themselves to be victims if they do not assert themselves. Action requires courage to change what can and needs to be changed. If you have been wronged, it will require concerted effort to free yourself from your bondage to the anger and extend yourself in mercy and love. To live according to your values, you must act on them. To grow as a person, you must live your values.

The third discipline is awareness that is clear and accurate. The line between what you can and cannot change is often unclear. You will need to observe with an open mind, putting aside your fixed ideas and judgments. Clear discernment will require you to distinguish your perceptions of reality and your prejudiced interpretations of it. You tell yourself many stories about how you want your life to be and ignore how it is. Clear awareness leads to wisdom and the freedom to act effectively.

Your anger is a vital energy. It can destroy or build up. It can produce life or death. Working the steps will enable you to use that energy with wisdom and compassion. Your efforts can set you free from your addiction to anger and develop a forgiving heart.

6

Admitting Your Powerlessness:
Toward Acceptance

Step One: "We admitted our powerlessness over our anger—
that our lives had become unmanageable."

"There is something powerful in being rendered powerless.
It will break your arrogance and possibly set you free."

—Mooji

I awakened when I admitted I was in trouble. I remember the precise day, time, and place. It was Easter afternoon at a family party. Born into a good Catholic family, we go to church and celebrate the holy days. We had just remembered Jesus' passion and death on the cross, and that day we celebrated the new life of the resurrection. At the family gathering, as usual, there was an abundance of food and drinks. Both were consumed excessively. As the afternoon and the drinking wore on, the noise level and obnoxious bantering increased. That day, for some reason, the alcoholic chaos I had experienced countless times got under my skin. It invaded my calm. I simmered with rage. "Not again," I shouted to myself. To keep from exploding and falling apart, I sneaked out of the house for a walk. "How could they all be so out of control, so crazy?" I repeated to myself. Then, a light went on, and I said, "How could I be so out of control? I have a problem. I need help." That moment set me on the road to recovery.

Step one invites you to take the first leap of faith: Embrace the pain of your anger and your powerlessness. As the AA Big Book warns, that is something that is contrary to our natural desires. Who wants to embrace pain and accept powerlessness? Especially if you are prone to anger, you relish the momentary feeling of power it offers. Who wants to give that up?

Accepting pain and powerlessness goes against the grain. One patient told me, "As a man, I've been taught all my life that I should be strong and in control of my life. I took pride in standing up for myself. Now, after all these years, you're telling me I should become powerless. That's ridiculous." Another patient, who had been abused as a child and in her marriage, complained, "I had to be strong to leave my husband. It saved my life. The idea of accepting my powerlessness repulses me. It puts me back into that familiar place of being a victim."

Power Hungry

Those addicted to anger resist this first step for an additional reason. They crave power, control, and perfection. Bill Wilson, the cofounder of AA, observed that the heart of any addiction is the desire to "play God." Whether addicted to a substance, a mood, or a way of thinking, they want complete control over their lives. Like God, they fantasize about being all-knowing, all-powerful, and perfect. They believe they can manage life at their convenience, make the world dance to their tune. They become control freaks. There are several areas where they attempt to exert control, but end up destined to defeat.

First of all, if you have an anger sickness, you may wish to have absolute control over your thoughts and feelings. You wish you could turn them on and off at your whim. At times, the anger makes you feel powerful. At other times, your preoccupation with the hurt and revenge drains you. When you feel stuck, powerless to control them, you desperately try harder to make your mind and emotions submit.

Whenever I begin therapy with a new patient, I always ask, "What made you decide to come and see me?" Invariably, the person tells me about their problem, all their failed efforts to fix it, and their sense of being defeated. I then ask them, "What would you like to accomplish by our meeting?"

Again, the predictable response, "I want to feel better. I want to get rid of my temper, learn how to control it." Those who have swallowed their anger say, "I want to get rid of my fear so I can stand up for myself."

I then explain, "You can't just get rid of your unpleasant thoughts and feelings. They just happen as automatic reactions. Besides, getting rid of them is an act of violence against yourself. It's a battle that will only harm you, and you cannot win. Your thoughts and feelings are natural. They are your friends who bring you an important message. Let's try to listen to them." My comment makes them pause to reflect with a large measure of disbelief.

I add, "Your thoughts and feelings are like clouds that come and go. They come from you, but they are not you. You are the blue sky." I explain that their consciousness is like the sky, an open space with many passing mental events. Hopefully, their confusion makes them curious to learn more about how their minds work.

Next, when you look in the mirror, what do you see? Be honest with yourself about the thoughts that flow through your mind. You may see facial features that remind you of your parents, hating the receding hairline and double chin. You may wish you had control over many of the circumstances of your life and your own biology. You may imagine that if you were born into a healthy family with perfect parents you would be happy. You may further imagine that if you had different physical, emotional, or temperamental characteristics you would be content. Perhaps you believe that more money, success, status, or power would bring happiness. The list of the circumstances that define your life are endless, and largely beyond your control.

Thirdly, you may dwell on your past and wish it had been different. A patient of mine who struggled with his temper said, "I have recurring dreams of being trapped. I try with all my might to get out of this closed in place, but cannot escape. I often dwell on the past, how my parents hurt me and how I was mistreated on a job I grew to hate."

"What do you think the dream is about?" I asked.

"I have so many regrets about my past and often wonder what my life would be like if only I had acted differently. I believe I'm a prisoner of my past. I can't escape it, and I hate that I'm powerless over it," he replied.

I suggested, "What would happen if you accepted the past and tried to see how it shaped your life and even helped make you the strong person you are today?"

Fourthly, you may wish you could change other people. You may imagine that if other people treated you the way you wanted to be treated you would be happy. You may expend much energy manipulating and coercing them to behave as you would like. Predictably, they resent your efforts to change them, just as you would.

When I meet with couples who are stuck in a power struggle, I ask each of them what would make them happy in their marriage. The wife may say, "I wish my husband would pay more attention to me, be less preoccupied with work, and include me in decision-making. I want us to be a team." The husband may say, "I wish my wife would nag me less, give me more sex, and give me space."

I then would point out, "Isn't it interesting that both of you imagine you would be happy if the other person changed the way you want them to change? Do you see what you both are doing? You are making your happiness dependent on someone else changing. You are making your partner responsible for your emotional well-being." I would then suggest shifting their focus from the other to themselves, asking, "What do you need to do to make yourself happy and the kind of partner you want to be?" Clearly, mature love can only be freely given when both parties are free to be themselves.

In your craving for power, control, and perfection, you live in a fantasy world without even knowing it. Your life is guided by the delusion that if you could control your unpleasant thoughts and feelings, your life circumstances, your past, and other people, then you would be happy. Your life would be complete. Unaware of your self-created predicament, you have dug a mental hole for yourself and are in freefall. You will not wake up until you hit the rock hard bottom of reality. The unavoidable collision with reality will shatter your illusions and invite you to let them go. Only then will you be free to be yourself.

Unmanageable Lives: Victims of Your Own Temper

Your excessive anger will precipitate distressful collisions with reality. I tell my patients, "No one gives up an addiction until they personally realize that the trouble it causes outweighs the benefits." Your anger addiction gives you a benefit. If you direct your temper outward, you feel powerful and may get your way. If you direct your anger inward, you can withdraw from life and responsibilities. However, whether under-controlled or over-controlled, you pay a severe price. AA warns about the "fatal nature of the situation" with uncontrolled resentment. Anger is counted as one of the seven deadly sins because of the deadly consequences of its inappropriate expression. An AA saying states, "If you want to bury someone with revenge, it is best to dig two graves."

Leonard, victimized by his temper:

> *"I hate my anger. It's like a snowball rolling down a mountain. Once it gains momentum, there's nothing I can do about it. When someone offends me, I can't get it out of my mind. I think about the hurt constantly and about getting revenge. I can't sleep at night. I'm so tense. I'm so distracted that I can't concentrate on anything but how I was wronged. It drives me insane."*

Loretta, allowing herself to be victimized:

> *"I let people take advantage of me, and I hate myself for it. It's just so scary for me to speak up for myself. I'm afraid of offending people and of them getting angry with me. I never say 'no' and often feel overwhelmed. I'm so depressed."*

Your excessive reactions to the natural energy of anger affect your whole person. It has emotional, physical, spiritual, and relationship consequences. Pay attention to how you are a victim of your own temper, whether directed outward or inward:

Emotional consequences:

- Shame and guilt for your temper outbursts.

- Depression, holding your anger in.

- Emotional exhaustion.

- Strong feelings of loneliness and isolation.

- Low self-esteem and sense of helplessness.

Physical consequences:

- Difficulty sleeping.

- Feeling burned out.

- Physical injuries from fighting or reckless behavior.

- Medical problems, such as high blood pressure, ulcers, stomach problems, etc.

- Chronic muscular tension.

Spiritual consequences:

- Feeling hopeless and despairing.

- Anger at God.

- Feeling disconnected from yourself and others.
- Loss of faith.

Relationship consequences:

- Injuring those closest to you.
- Estrangement from family and friends.
- Marital strife.
- Decreased productivity at work.
- Job loss, legal problems, financial problems, jail.

Unmanageable Lives: Victims of Others' Tempers

Your anger is not only self-defeating. You may have been defeated by the anger of those close to you. The deep wounds fester and color your view of the world and yourself. Your own anger may cover over traumas from early life, all the hurt, shame, and fear. Furthermore, you may lack positive role models for the appropriate expression of anger.

Marion, a victim of childhood abuse:

"My wife tells me I'm just like my father. I hate it when she says that because I despised the man. He used to beat me for no reason and call me names. I never do that with my kids. I admit I have a temper, but I've learned to control myself. When I get angry, I shake all over and clench my fists, but I'm never violent. My wife tells me the children are afraid of me. She says I'm a perfectionist and can be overly demanding of them. I guess that's true, but I think I'm doing it for their own good. She says I go overboard and become too judgmental."

Look back on your own life and the impact of angry people on your wellbeing. Someone taught you how to manage your anger. You may see more clearly the consequences of your own unrestrained anger in other people more than in yourself. Ask yourself the following questions to begin the personal exploration of your own anger:

- How was anger expressed by your parents? What was their anger style?
- What were the messages you received from your family about expressing anger?
- How were you disciplined as a child? Was it excessive?
- Were you rewarded or punished for the way you expressed your anger?
- How have you been the victim of others' tempers?
- Have you been a scapegoat, often unfairly blamed?

- Do you often feel judged by others?

- How did you react to being mistreated?

Dante's *Inferno*, written in the 14th century, graphically portrays the impact of anger, either indulged or suppressed. Anger outward is called "wrath," while inward anger is labeled "sullenness." Those whose lives were dominated by anger reside in the fifth circle of hell. They thrash about in the stinking black sludge of the river Styx, "choking on their own venom." Naked and muddy, the wrathful furiously attack each other. The sullen stew below the surface of the muddy swamp, bubbles rising to the surface as the only sign of life. They are powerless to escape their miserable fate.

Power of Personal Responsibility

Aware of where you are powerless and the consequences of your misguided efforts at control, what, then, do you have power over in your life? What can you manage effectively? Defeat shocks you. It can bring you to the brink of despair, or it can jolt you to look deeply within yourself to discover where your true freedom and power lie. Where are you free?

If you look closely at your experience, you will discover that you are truly free in three areas. First, you have control over your attention. You can choose what thoughts and feelings to dwell on and how much weight to give them. You may claim a lack of will power and say to yourself, "I have no control over my mind. I can't help stewing about things." That is not true. Thoughts and feelings are like passing clouds, weightless mist, that cannot command your attention. With practice, you can train your mind to be selective.

Secondly, you can choose your attitude toward your thoughts and feelings and what happens to you. You may blame outside influences for your reactions and object, "I hate my job. It makes me feel so miserable. My coworkers also make me so angry. I can't help it." Again, that is not true. Circumstances, other people, and even your own mental reactions have no more power over your life than you give them. You are free to assume any attitude, positive or negative, that benefits you. That also requires practice.

Viktor Frankl, a concentration camp survivor, affirmed this basic freedom to choose one's attitude even in the most extreme circumstances. He claimed that we can assert our will to live under any conditions if we have a "why." Discovering personal meaning provides the strength to endure. He said, "Everything can be taken from a man but one thing: the last of human freedoms—to choose one's attitude in any given set of circumstances, to choose one's own way."

Finally, you are able to choose how to act. You may blame your personality and protest, "I'm an angry person. That's who I am. That's how I'm built. I have no control over myself." Again, not true.

I tell my patients, "Your anger does not define you as a person. It is a momentary experience you have. Anger, like all feelings, comes and goes. You don't have to act on every urge." If you become more conscious of your behavior, you can choose to change it.

The blame game never works. It only makes you feel more helpless, more like a victim.

The book of Chinese wisdom, *Tao Te Ching*, expresses clearly the power of personal responsibility learned through failure:

Failure is an opportunity.
If you blame someone else,
there is no end to the blame.

Therefore, the Master
fulfills her own obligations
and corrects her own mistakes.
She does what she needs to do
and demands nothing of others (79).

In the midst of your failure and sense of powerlessness to manage your anger, you have a choice. You can give up in despair and blame others, your circumstances, or fate for your misery. You can choose to remain a victim. Or you can shift the focus to yourself and take responsibility for your own life. You can stop blaming, demanding, and expecting to be rescued. You can look seriously at your own life, over which you have power, and make decisions based on your deepest desires and true values. Embracing your weakness, you find the strength to grow up.

Watch the Waterfall

To begin the process of being aware of their own experience and taking personal responsibility for their responses, I invite my patients to use their imagination. I tell them, "Imagine your stream of consciousness, the continuous flow of thoughts and feelings, as a waterfall. You can respond in a few different ways to the flow. You can try to stop it, jump into the river, or watch it." Let me explain.

First, you can try to stop the flow, by ignoring it or distracting yourself with other thoughts and activities when you feel a hostile impulse, but the pressure builds, and the unwanted thoughts, feelings, and impulses erupt with a vengeance or seep through in indirect ways, influencing your behavior without your awareness. What you resist persists.

The second approach is to jump into the stream of consciousness, give up any effort to manage the flow, and risk drowning. In the midst of an anger attack, you feel powerless to resist the urgent rush of threatening thoughts and feelings and are overwhelmed. The impulse to retaliate seems irresistible. You get carried away against your will.

The third approach, the only really effective one, is to become an observer of the flow of your thoughts, feelings, and physical sensations. It is like standing back and watching a waterfall, without trying to dam it or jump in. With practice, you can learn to become an astute observer of yourself and the ongoing flow. Taking in the information, you become acquainted with how your mind works. You gain valuable information so you can decide how to act in your best interest. The more you practice observing, the more you develop habit strength to transform your life.

Pain Teaches

When you observe closely your experience with anger, you will notice the pain it causes. Your natural instinct is to seek pleasure and avoid pain, at nearly all costs. The first step, like all the steps, asks you to act contrary to your natural desires. You want to avoid and rid yourself of the discomfort your anger, either indulged or suppressed, causes you. Much to their surprise, I invite my patients, "Lean into your pain. Don't avoid it. Learn its message."

As much as you want to avoid feeling the pain, imagine what your life would be like if you never felt pain?

Initially, you might think it would be heaven on earth, a dream realized. Your life would proceed pleasantly without the distraction of pain—until you injure yourself. You might not even notice when you hurt yourself because you feel no pain to alert you. You may not seek treatment. The cut may become infected, and eventually cost you a limb, or worse, your life. You may become afflicted with an infinite variety of illnesses and not even know it. Without treatment, the simple sickness could become complex, damaging vital organs, and, again, costing you your life. You ignore the signs at your own peril.

Physical pain, as much as you hate it, serves a survival purpose. It alerts you to an injury that requires attention. Pain grabs your attention and launches you on an exploratory search to find its cause. When you clearly understand the cause, you can move towards the proper remedy.

Emotional pain serves a similar survival purpose, to protect your psychological wellbeing. When you feel anxious, depressed, or angry, it is a warning sign that something is out of balance in your life. Of course, you hate the discomfort of these feelings and wish they would magically disappear, but these emotional reactions are symptoms of some deeper problem that is calling out for attention. Neglecting to address that deeper problem can put your long-term happiness at risk. Taking the pain seriously and exploring the causes can lead to growth.

Imagine that your hand is frostbitten. It is numb. You feel no pain. However, as your hand begins to thaw, you feel excruciating pain. You think your condition is worsening, but actually, you are in the process of healing. In the same way, when you fully feel your anger and the fear and hurt that underlie it, you are beginning to heal. Sometimes my patients complain, "I felt better when I started therapy, but now I feel worse."

I assure them, "Your pain is a sign that you are coming alive. When you feel nothing, you are dead."

Your anger alerts you that some important need is not being met. There is an obstacle to your wellbeing that you have to overcome. You may feel wronged, wounded, mistreated. The anger is a call to action, energizing you to protect yourself. Unless you have a clear understanding of the real danger and assess the best course of action, your anger can be like a misguided missile. It can wreak destruction on yours and others' lives, but anger well used can help you grow.

Power Of Acceptance

I go the gym several times a week. As I enter the place, a poster greets me with a picture of a young, fit, attractive woman. In bold print, an inscription reads, "I can do it all in my lifetime." That message may motivate me to push myself hard, but it may also lead me to the despair of expecting too much. Your problem begins with the craving for power, control, and perfection. You have an agenda you may even be hiding from yourself. Often, unrealistic expectations drive that agenda. Society encourages us to aim high, often too high.

Emotions Anonymous, an outgrowth of AA, alerts us to the danger of inflated expectations: "In our search for self-worth and identity, we may have unknowingly set unrealistic goals for ourselves. Because our ideals are too high and we can never live up to these unrealistic expectations, our sense of self-worth is low. How can we but fail" (1). Striving for perfection, to play God, sets us up for disappointment and resentment. To compensate for our sense of failure, we become power hungry, pushing ourselves and others harder. We become like Sisyphus, condemned to push a boulder up a mountain over and over only to have it role back down.

How can you escape this treadmill of despair? Freedom comes only from accepting your lack of power, your imperfections, and your limitations. The Navajo Indians, who are well-known for their expertise in rug making, have a practice of always weaving an imperfection into the corner. The design pattern is perfect, except for this one obvious flaw. The Indians explain this intended mistake is the place where the Spirit moves in and out of the rug. Leonard Cohen makes the same point in a refrain from his song "Anthem," "There is a crack in everything. That's how the light gets in." True perfection comes from accepting imperfections, all the cracks and flaws.

Paradox of Weakness and Strength

Alcoholics Anonymous offers many slogans for recovery that provoke an alternative consciousness and way of living. They affirm that you can change your life by changing your thinking. These slogans express a hidden wisdom in a surprising way that contradicts your ordinary one-track thinking. They are called paradoxes, which means, "a union of opposites." What you think cannot go together is really intimately related if you look more deeply. Paradoxes invite you to see wholeness, rather than contradictions, in the world around you. They challenge your usual 'either-or' thinking to see more inclusively, in 'both-and' terms.

Step one suggests the paradox: "From weakness comes strength." Within weakness is found the seed of strength, just as strength foreshadows weakness. Weakness and strength are really two sides of the same coin. You do not have to despise your anger, which only keeps you in the merry-go-round of hate and rejection. Instead, accepting your powerlessness over your excessive anger opens the door to new life. Pain propels you to undertake a personal journey in search of healing and growth. The suffering, if accepted, opens your heart to personal responsibility and compassion for yourself and others.

In the Christian tradition, St. Paul offers a model of a powerful embracing of weakness (II Corinthians 12: 7-10). He complained of having a terrible, "thorn in the flesh," that he considered a beating from an angel of Satan. Paul does not specify the nature of this suffering, only his powerlessness to find relief. He begged God to remove this pain, but his prayers were answered in an unexpected way. The Lord said to him, "My grace is enough for you, for in weakness power reaches perfection." Paul then accepted his weaknesses, even boasted about them, "that the power of Christ may rest upon me." Through his suffering, he gave up his pride and self-sufficiency, finding his strength in God, a Power greater than himself.

Practice: Follow the Breath

Now it is time to turn these ideas into habits, into ways of living. Don't think, just look. As many spiritual teachers suggest, become like a polished mirror that reflects the truth and beauty of the world. Remove the specks of dust that cloud the mirror and distort the image reflected. The dust specks that become as thick as mud are your fixed opinions, biased judgments, and misguided expectations.

Without realizing it, your distorted thinking causes you all your trouble. You create a world in your mind that does not correspond with reality. You entertain fantastic expectations of how life should be. The disappointment you suffer when your experience does not match your expectations fuels your rage. Your anger then propels you to change the world, take control, and make everything conform to your agenda. Tragically, if your rage is unchecked, it will consume you.

To help release you from the bondage to your thinking, you need to practice looking without thinking or judging. You cannot stop your active mind, but you can learn to let the thoughts come and go, like clouds in the spacious sky. Following your breath is a practice to help you disengage from your thought prison. It is an eastern practice called "Samadhi," which means, "abiding in peace" (2). It will help you become an observer of your experience, and not a manipulator of it. In this exercise, you follow your breath because it keeps you in the present moment and connects you with your body and the outer world. The word "breath" also means "spirit," which immerses you in the Real.

The practice is simple, yet powerful:

1. Find a quiet place, away from as many distractions as possible. Sit in a relaxed position with your back erect and your head straight. You may sit in a chair with your feet firmly planted on the ground and hands on your lap, palms facing upward in a position of receiving a gift. You may prefer to sit in the traditional lotus position, with your legs crossed, but that is not necessary. Whatever your preferred posture, feel as though you are grounded. Keep your eyes closed to avoid distractions. Begin with the intention to pay full attention only to your breath.

2. Next, breathe deeply from your abdomen. It is important to breathe deeply, from the center of your body, and not in a shallow manner as you do when anxious or depressed. Breathe regularly and sense the fresh air filling all parts of your body. Scan your body and notice the areas of tension. Consciously send your breath to those areas and feel the warmth of your breath bring relaxation. Let the frozen tension melt away. Breathe slowly and regularly, not quickly and unsteadily. Find comfort in the regularity of your slow, deep breathing.

3. Now focus all your attention on the rising and falling of your breath. You may begin by counting your breaths and noticing the gap between inhaling and exhaling. Follow the sensation of your breathing and the moving of your body from your stomach, through your chest and windpipe, and out your nose. Become body-conscious. Soon you will notice intrusive thoughts and other sensations that distract you from attending fully to your breath. Your racing mind wants to take over, but resist the urge, and return to your breath.

4. When you are distracted by thoughts and other sensations, gently let them go. Do not dwell on them as you usually do. Return your attention to your breath. Also, avoid struggling with the thoughts. Do not try to get rid of them, as you often do when the thoughts are unpleasant. Simply acknowledge their presence and continue following your breath.

Practice this procedure every day to make it a habit. You can begin with a five-minute practice and gradually extend the time as you become more comfortable with it. You also can do this exercise at any time and in any place for brief periods, especially when you are feeling agitated.

Pain and powerlessness push you to take the first step towards healing and growth. "No pain, no gain," many physical therapists tell their clients. The same holds true with emotional/spiritual healing. Coming to acceptance and full responsibility for your anger sickness prepares you for the next step into an encounter with mystery. Anthony Paul Moo-Young, known as Mooji, is a Jamaican spiritual master. Truth-seekers from around the world gather at his home in Portugal to hear his words of wisdom. He taught, "We are both human and divine. Human troubles compelled the wise to discover their divine nature."

Dennis Ortman, Ph.D.

7

Trust in a Power Greater:
Surrendering Self-Will

Step Two: "We came to believe that a Power greater than ourselves could restore us to sanity."

Step Three: "Made a decision to turn our will and our lives over to the care of God as we understood Him."

"No problem can be solved by the same consciousness that caused the problem in the first place."

—Albert Einstein

I was raised Catholic in a restless, exciting time when the Church was in the midst of a long-overdue transition. American society reflected the tumult. It was the 1960s. The Second Vatican Council opened the Church's windows, letting in a breath of fresh air. Many applauded the changes, while others were appalled by them. John Kennedy inspired Camelot, which tragically ended with his assassination. Millions took to the streets to protest the Vietnam War. Martin Luther King cried freedom for the oppressed blacks and shared his dream. The questioning spirit of the time challenged my childlike, comfortable faith. I learned to pray and believe in ways I never anticipated. The God of my childhood was an insecure refuge. I needed a new God. I could only surrender to the new life that was unfolding.

Steps two and three invite you to surrender, taking another leap of faith: Trust in a Power greater than yourself. In making this leap, you step back to reflect on your faith, then forward to make a decision. The spirit of the times today makes the decision of faith daunting. The seeds of discontent planted in the 1960s have come again to fruition. Many question the value of institutional religion, preferring to call themselves "spiritual" rather than "religious." The language, dogmas, and practices of traditional religion no longer satisfy our deep spiritual needs. Many of us have become solitary seekers, longing to discover what is of ultimate concern for us.

Alcoholics Anonymous has been sensitive to the currents of religious questioning. Nevertheless, it has insisted on the power of an authentic spirituality to effect personal healing and growth. Its members attest to the power of faith to change their lives. An AA slogan states, "Religion is for people who are afraid of hell. Spirituality is for people who have been there." Your anger throws you down into hell. The acceptance of your powerlessness lifts your heart in hope for new life.

Coming to Believe

We are heirs today of the critical, questioning spirit of the 1960s regarding religion. Recent polls document the severity of the crisis of faith and religion (1). Almost a fifth (16 to 20 percent) declare themselves unaffiliated with any church or having no religion. Many are either agnostics or atheists, and some say they are "spiritual." The young are especially skeptical. Between 25 and 30 percent of adults under age thirty claim no religious affiliation. America's third largest religious group currently is composed of those who profess no faith. Even those who belong to a church do not practice regularly. Only about 20 percent of Americans attend weekly services, and the same small percentage say they have a "great deal" of confidence in organized religion.

Many of my patients express this skepticism about traditional religion. They exhibit a rugged individualism in their personal searches for meaning, for something more, something new to guide their lives. Here is a sample of what I hear, followed by my description of true believing:

"I hate the arrogance of so many religious people. They think they have all the answers. They think they have a corner on the truth and try to convert you to their way of thinking."

Faith invites you to look deeper, beneath the surface of everyday life. Believing draws you into the darkness of the unknown, which is beyond your understanding and control, but from which all knowing arises. It is a journey to the Center and Source of life, which is shrouded in mystery. Despite the apparent clarity of Bible and Church teachings, you cannot reduce the mystery of life into what you can manageably know.

"I have a bumper sticker on my car: 'RELIGION—because thinking is hard.' People accept a blind faith because they don't want to use their brains. They want something simple, superstitious, and magical."

Faith does not contradict reason or science, but you cannot reason yourself to believe. The mystery of faith goes beyond the thinking mind and engages you at a deeper level. You believe with your whole person, your mind, heart, and soul. It requires a wholehearted trust, a heart-consciousness that engages you at the core of your being. Furthermore, faith is not an alternative to science or reason. Rather, it is enriched by both.

"So many church goers have a simple answer for everything. They just look up something in the Bible that tells them what to do. They're so narrow-minded. You can't argue with them."

Genuine faith opens, not closes, your mind. It involves a journey to a sunlit mountain-top where you can see forever. It is a new state of consciousness open to the fullness of life, where you see that everything belongs. Nothing is excluded. Even what you fear and despise can be incorporated into your path to a wholesome life.

"I don't believe in simply waiting for happiness in the next life, waiting for the rewards of heaven. That just seems like an escape."

True faith is not an escape from this world, but an invitation to be responsible to create a better world. Believing involves being fully engaged in the present moment, which reveals the divine presence. It means taking this life seriously, making this world a better place, as the path to happiness. The eternal is found in the everyday, here, now. Jesus said, "The kingdom of God is at hand."

"Some of the so-called religious I meet think they are 'holier than thou.' They think that by simply saying, 'Jesus is my Lord,' that they are saved."

Authentic faith is more about actions than words. It is embracing a way of life guided by a belief in the Ultimate Source of Love. The Dalai Lama expressed this beautifully when he said, "My religion is kindness." Genuine faith overflows in a life of virtue, which is its true mark.

"I'm absolutely scandalized by how the Catholic Church covered up the sexual abuse of children by priests. The mistreatment of women also disgusts me. I can't tolerate the hypocrisy."

Faith is in God, not the Church. Unfortunately, many Church members, including its leaders, have not lived up to ideals they proclaim. All churches are composed of sinners, who hopefully desire to be saints. Churches are only imperfect vehicles to carry its members to the further shore of holiness and enlightenment. The Church only points the way to God in whom we place our trust.

"Those who are born again claim they are saved. They see themselves as God's elect, destined for heaven. What makes them better than any of us?"

Coming to believe is a lifelong journey that is never complete. It begins with the desire to believe and may take many twists and turns before you arrive at a decision of faith. That decision will deepen over time as your faith is challenged to grow through suffering in new situations. It grows as you gradually let go of your selfish desires and let God in.

True believing concerns:

- The unknown, not the known.
- The heart, not only the head.
- Opening, not closing, the mind.
- Here and now, not then and there.
- A lifestyle, not a belief system.
- Believing in God, not being a church member.
- A life-long journey, not a final destination.

Sweet Surrender

The decision of faith requires turning your will and life over to God. The first key ingredient is willingness to surrender. What do you surrender when you believe? You give up your insistence that you will only live on your own terms. "Not my will, but yours be done," faith says. You give up your protest in the midst of adversity, "I don't want it to be this way." To make such a radical surrender of your will, you must let go of all your programs for happiness, your beliefs that you will find lasting satisfaction in power, prestige, or possessions. You cannot even hang on to your image of God, which is a vain attempt to limit and control Him. To let God into your life, you must let go of all your self-centered desires, even your anger. That is a life-long task.

Mario, letting go of a grudge:

"I was deeply offended by my cousin many years ago. I promised I would never speak to him again, and I was true to my word. Anger consumed me so much that I could not go to church. Any sermons that suggested forgiveness made me sick. Everything changed when I heard that my cousin was dying of cancer. I thought, "Good. That SOB deserves it." My wife pleaded with me to visit him in the hospital before he died. I finally relented. When I went to see him, he was in so much pain he could not talk. He only grabbed my hand and cried. I cried with him. The next Sunday, I went back to church."

Only great suffering or great love can move us to surrender our self will. Only then can we let in the light of faith and experience its sweetness.

Everything within you protests against such a surrender of your will if you suffer from an anger sickness. Alcoholics Anonymous states, in no uncertain terms, the root cause of your anger addiction, "Our whole trouble had been the misuse of willpower. We had tried to bombard our problems with it instead of attempting to bring it into agreement with God's intention for us" (Steps/Traditions, p. 40). Prone to anger, you cling to high expectations about how life should be. You use your anger to manage and manipulate the environment to conform to your will.

A second key ingredient of faith, in addition to surrender, is trust. You must be willing to ask for and accept help to have faith. You can only believe in a God you view as trustworthy, certain to be there for you. However, your anger may reveal your reluctance to trust, to depend on anyone but yourself. That is why you crave control so much. You may have felt betrayed by important people in your life, such as your parents. You did not believe you could rely on and ask them for help. Consequently, you found refuge in yourself, building walls of hatred to protect yourself. You may only be able to trust in a Greater Power as these wounds heal.

One patient told me, "My parents were brutal, and they forced us to go to church. It was hard for me to believe in a loving and merciful God. I experienced so little mercy in my life. When the minister talked about God as a loving Father, I cringed."

Where's the Power

Where do you find the Power greater than yourself to believe in? Step three makes a crucial point when it speaks about God with the distinction, "as you understand Him." It separates your personal experience of God, on the one hand, and your understanding of Him, on the other. Personal experience and understanding are not the same thing.

The steps encourage you also to undertake a personal search for God (or Truth) and to look to your experience. For authentic faith, you cannot rely on any church's teachings, the opinions of others, or even the guidance of someone in authority. They can only point a way. You have to trust yourself. You need to take personal responsibility to discover what gives ultimate meaning to your life and to put your faith in that. There is no simple end to this search that any religion can ratify. Gandhi said, "In reality, there are as many religions as there are individuals."

The personal search for a Power greater than yourself, which you may call God, involves an encounter with Mystery. All the religious traditions underline the Mystery of the Divine, the gap that can only be bridged by faith. The *Tao Te Ching*, the book of ancient Chinese wisdom, teaches in the opening verse: "The tao (god) that can be told is not the eternal Tao (God), the name that can be named is not the eternal Name." Whatever you think or say about God does not adequately reflect the fullness of His reality. Buddhists remind us that all our talk about ultimate reality, "is not the moon, only a finger pointing to the moon." Saint Paul instructs, "Now we are seeing a dim reflection in a mirror; but then we shall be seeing face to face" (I Cor 13:12). You approach the Divine Mystery with humility, acknowledging the limitations of your understanding.

Nevertheless, your faith seeks some understanding. You want to give your God a name. Opinions vary on how you imagine God and where you find him. Recent research shows that Americans think differently about God. Ninety two percent claim that they believe in God. However, the way they think about the Divinity varies. Sixty percent view God as a person, while twenty five percent consider God an impersonal force in the universe. Seven percent say it is impossible to know anything about God (2).

Like most Americans, you may think of God as personal, impersonal, unknowable, or even nonexistent. Where do you look to find the Divine Power for your life?" You can look in three directions:

- Beyond—towards a personal God, the Supreme Being.

- Around—towards the Life Force within the universe.

- Within—towards your Higher Consciousness.

A Personal God

Traditional religion invites you to believe in a personal Supreme Being. God is the Creator, Redeemer, and Sanctifier. He dwells in the heavens and rules the universe. Of course, the crucial question for you as a believer is, "What is God's attitude toward me?" Again, a recent Baylor University study of college students (Bass, p. 49) suggested that believers perceive His character differently. The study indicated that thirty one percent believed in an authoritarian God who is judging and wrathful. Twenty three percent professed faith in a benevolent, forgiving God. Sixteen percent viewed God as critical, but just, while twenty four percent considered God distant, uninvolved.

Whether you view God as judging, forgiving, critical, or uninvolved can affect how your faith benefits your emotional wellbeing. Your self-image and notion of God mutually influence each other. While you were taught that you were created, "in the image and likeness of God," you tend to create God in your own image. What you see in yourself, you project onto God. If you are consumed by anger, your God will be angry and wrathful. In turn, that image will reinforce your hostile attitude and fear of judgment.

Abigail, an insecure believer:

> "I was raised in a strict Christian home. We knew what was right and wrong, and my parents enforced all the rules. At times I hated the discipline, but I knew it was good for me. We went to church as a family three times a week and studied the Bible together. At church the pastor gave fire-and-brimstone sermons that scared me. I had visions of the hell fire and was terrified of God punishing me for even the smallest offenses. Now, at thirty years old, I'm in therapy for an anxiety condition."

Coming to believe in a loving, forgiving God will heal the wound of your sorrow-bearing wrath. AA portrays the Higher Power as loving and caring, Someone to call upon in need. The Christian and Islamic Scriptures proclaim God mostly as forgiving and merciful. Unfortunately, as research indicates, only a minority view their God in such positive terms. Perhaps our aggressive culture leaves a stronger imprint on our religious views than the teachings of the churches.

A Life Force

Those of a scientific bent may prefer to look at the world around them in search of that Power greater than themselves. They are predisposed to view their God as a Life Force that pervades the universe. Bill Wilson, the cofounder of Alcoholics Anonymous, thought of God in impersonal terms. He wrote:

> "The word God still aroused a certain antipathy. When the thought was expressed that there might be a God personal to me, this feeling intensified. I didn't like the idea. I could go for such conceptions as Creative Intelligence, Universal Mind or Spirit of Nature, but I resisted the thought of a Czar of the Heavens, however loving His sway might be. I have since talked with scores of men who felt the same way" (4).

As with faith in a personal God, if you entrust yourself to the care of an impersonal Life Force, you need to address the question that Einstein poses: "The most important decision we make is whether we believe in a friendly or hostile universe." What do you believe about the ultimate value, meaning, and purpose of the universe? Science cannot answer this question. It is a matter of personal faith. There is no rational proof, but plenty of evidence to support either choice. Believing the universe hostile encourages pessimism, paranoia, and despair about life. Believing in its friendliness inspires optimism, openness, and joy. It also inspires confidence in your own goodness.

Power and Presence

A third place to look for the Power greater than yourself is within yourself. Disillusioned with institutional religions and their ancient myths, many prefer to look inward. In your personal search for Truth, you may examine closely your own experiences and listen to your deepest longings.

There is a story about spiritual seeking in Swami Muktananda's book, *Kundalini; The Secret of Life,* related by Christina Grof (5):

Before the creation of the world, God existed alone. After a while, He became lonely and bored and wanted someone to play with. So God created the world and lesser gods to help him run it. All the creatures knew they were divine because they came from God. They also knew how to merge back to their source in God. After a short time, the creatures lost interest in the world and ventured back to God in heaven. God's game was over, and He was bored again.

God called a council of the lesser gods and asked for their advice to renew the game. One suggested, "Why not toss everyone out of heaven, lock the gates, and throw away the key? Then erect veils of forgetfulness so that these beings cannot easily remember where they came from?"

God thought it was an excellent idea and asked, "Where should we hide the key to heaven?"

"In the depths of the ocean," one god suggested.

"No, at the top of the highest mountain," another said.

"Let's put it on the moon, so far away no one will ever reach it," offered a third god.

God sat in meditation to consider their suggestions. Discouraged, he said to them, "None of these ideas will work. Humans are ingenious. They will explore the far reaches of the universe. They will dive to the bottom of the deepest ocean and climb the highest mountain. They will visit the moon, explore other planets, and seek to understand the workings of the universe."

The gods listened in silence. Suddenly, God spoke, "I have an idea! I know the one place humans will not think of looking for the key to heaven. That place is within themselves, within their own hearts. They will travel millions of miles into space, but not venture to look within themselves to find the key to heaven." The gods all applauded God's brilliant plan. Since then, God has delighted in watching our search for the way home to Him.

Silence: The Gateway to Mystery

You may find God exploring the depths of your own consciousness. When you quiet your mind and listen in silence to what is inside you, what do you discover? You notice deep longings that come from no place you can identify. They arise from some void within you, from the depths of your unconscious. You are drawn to what is true, good, and beautiful. Have you ever wondered where an idea comes from, where the longings to love another arise, or how you freely make a decision? You sense a mysterious Power within you that animals and plants do not share. That Power is God-like in being creative, loving, and free. In the depths of our consciousness, we share in Divine Life. Perhaps that is what the Bible means when it says we are "made in the image and likeness of God."

In the stillness, you sense a Power and Presence you may call Divine. You sense it, but do not see it directly. Your perception of it is like a fish in water. The fish is totally immersed in water and does not even notice it. Sensing the Power and Presence is like feeling the air you breathe, invisible, essential to life, and noticed only when you see objects floating in it. You may note the rapid flow of your stream of consciousness with many thought objects floating in it. When you contemplate deeply, you are drawn to the source, the vast inexhaustible ocean, which is consciousness. Your consciousness, your pure awareness, participates in Divine Life.

The *Tao Te Ching* describes this process of opening self-consciousness. Being still, quieting your mind, you sense the hidden source of your being:

> Empty your mind of all thoughts.
> Let your heart be at peace.
> Watch the turmoil of beings,
> but contemplate their return.
> Each separate being in the universe
> returns to the common source.
> Returning to the source is serenity.
> If you don't realize the source,
> you stumble in confusion and sorrow (22).

Two Minds: Ordinary and Wise

When you observe closely the working of your mind, you notice two minds operating: the ordinary and the wise mind. On the one hand, the ordinary mind is constantly chattering, engaged in a mental dialogue that never stops. Many voices compete for attention and seem to outshout each other. Thoughts rise, fall, and clash with each other. This mind is sometimes called, "the wild monkey mind," because it jumps around. On the other hand, the wise mind rests and observes. It is the "you" that stands back and notices the incessant flow of thoughts and all the voices talking. It witnesses the story-telling and all the drama that results from it. It is you as the observing subject that can be sensed but not observed as an object.

With your wise mind, you observe the commotion of thoughts when possessed by anger. You notice a pattern in the thinking. It can be called the "mind of rejection," because it fights against reality. The ordinary mind of rejection has its own operating system:

- Has high expectations about how life should be.
- Is always judging and criticizing.
- Has an "us-against-them" mentality.
- Dwells on being wronged and hurts from the past.
- Sees enemies everywhere and imagines malevolent intentions.
- Is preoccupied with protecting itself and seeking revenge.
- Attacks first and asks questions later.

In contrast, the wise mind, which observes the drama of the mind of rejection, has a different operating system. It can be called the "mind of acceptance," because it takes a panoramic view and embraces the whole of reality. This higher consciousness has several qualities:

- Embraces life as it unfolds, without expectations.
- Observes without judging.
- Sees the big picture, that everything belongs.
- Engages the present moment fully.
- Has a friendly attitude toward all.
- Seeks to create unity.
- Loves first and last.

Taking the journey within, you realize that you are not the mind of rejection, with all the competing voices. You are the "one" who observes, the mind of acceptance. Your higher consciousness shares in Divinity so that, in knowing God, you know your true self, and in knowing your true self, you know God.

To Restore Sanity

If you learn to exercise your wise mind, the mind of acceptance, you discover who you really are. Beneath the turmoil of anxious, sad, and angry thoughts, you uncover what is hidden. You are strong, loving, and wise, essentially good. As Marcus Aurelius, the Roman philosopher-king, wrote in his *Meditations*, "Dig deep; the water—goodness—is down there. And as long as you keep digging, it will keep welling up" (6). Through ongoing practice in trusting your wise mind, you restore the sanity you already possess but overlook. You recover something that has been lost in your anger mania, your original sanity.

Patients come to me in distress, seeking to change what they do not like about themselves. They are surprised when I tell them my view of therapy. I explain, "Therapy is not a self-improvement project, about creating a better version of yourself. Instead, it is about allowing yourself simply to be yourself and removing any obstacles to you being your true self." Anger is one of the obstacles that need to be removed.

An AA saying states, "Insanity is doing the same thing over and over again, expecting a different result." Anger addicted, you dwell on the ways you have been wronged by individuals and even life itself. You rebel against the perceived unfairness. You attack those who attacked you, hoping that revenge will heal the wound, but it never works. The cycle of anger and violence escalates. You are a prisoner of the past, controlled by habitual aggressive reacting.

Instead, a different approach is suggested by the mind of acceptance—to let go of the anger and desire to retaliate. Martin Luther King expressed and modeled how to break the anger cycle: "Darkness cannot drive out darkness; only light can do that. Hate cannot drive out hate; only love can do that."

The Power greater than yourself, both within and beyond you, is your higher consciousness. That awareness seeks truth in love, which overcomes your anger addiction and restores you to sanity.

Paradox of Surrender and Victory

At his inaugural ball, Donald Trump chose a song for his first dance that caught everyone's attention. He chose a tune Frank Sinatra made famous, "I Did It My Way." That song expresses the rugged individualism that drove Trump's campaign and captured the imagination of many voters. "Make America Great Again," was a thread throughout his campaign speeches. He appealed to our natural instinct for power and control. Taking charge of our lives displays our strength of character, our determination, our will power. However, the second and third steps may shock you in their recommendation to exchange willfulness for willingness, to turn your life and will over to another. You may protest, "That's submission, allowing another to dominate me. I won't tolerate that!"

These steps propose a surprising paradox for recovery: "We surrender to win." What do you surrender and what do you win? As you observe your anger closely, you notice how it has taken over your life. Your excessive desires for control now control you. You may fearfully stuff or recklessly indulge it. In either case, it possesses you. You surrender your reliance on the illusory power of anger to advance your self-centered agenda. Glimpses of your character defects that underlie your anger begin to show. Those self-centered desires also need to be given up.

What do you win for the effort? You gain a sense of freedom to be yourself. Your anger and all your weaknesses over which you feel so powerless are like muddy water in a glass. When you quiet down to observe yourself and give up your agitated reacting, the mud settles to the bottom of the glass. The water is clear. It allows light to shine through. The clear water is you, and the light is your Higher Power. Surrendering your self-centered cravings, your true self shines forth. Mooji, the Jamaican spiritual master, describes what appears (7):

> Happiness is your nature,
> effortlessness is your dance.
> Peace is your fragrance,
> love is your perfume.

Practice: Insight Meditation

Cultivating the wise mind, the mind of acceptance, takes practice. As you observe the workings of your mind of rejection, you can begin to detach from its influence. A traditional eastern practice called Vipassana, which means, "insight meditation," can help you listen to the wondrous depths of your own consciousness. It is sometimes called "choiceless awareness," or, "bare awareness" (8). The purpose of the exercise is to help you connect with the vast openness of your consciousness. The procedure for this practice is simple, similar to the exercise of following your breath.

1) Find a quiet place. Assume a relaxed posture, with your back straight and head erect. You may sit on a chair with your feet on the floor or on a cushion in the lo-

tus position. Place your hands on your lap with the palms facing up in a receptive position. Keep your eyes open, focused on a spot in front of you.

2) Breathe deeply from your abdomen and follow your breath, as in the previous exercise. Feel the air filling the various parts of your body, relaxing all the tension in your muscles.

3) Begin with the conscious intention to be open to whatever arises in your consciousness. Welcome everything, the delightful and the unpleasant. Make the intention not to judge or reject whatever you experience.

4) As you quiet your mind and relax your body, notice the various thoughts, feelings, and sensations that arise. Note them and gently let go of them. Returning to your breath can help you hold the contents of your consciousness lightly. Just be an observer of all that comes and goes through your mind. Also pay attention to your spontaneous emotional reactions to the contents, whether you like, dislike, or are neutral to what you perceive. Notice what persists, tends to grab on to your awareness. Let that go also.

5) As you observe the flow of your consciousness, you can make a mental note of what you experience. Simply label a thought, feeling, or sensation, saying to yourself, "thought," "feeling," or "sensation." Do not ponder what you observe at this time.

6) After the meditation, take a few minutes to reflect on what you experienced. Take note of any powerful and repeating thoughts, feelings, and sensations.

Make this practice a daily habit, alternating it with the practice of following your breath. If the practice raises overwhelming traumatic memories, stop until you are ready to try again. Begin with a fifteen minute meditation and extend the time as you become more adept. Remember, practice does not make perfect, but makes for progress. You will need the strength and courage gained from trusting your Higher Power to undertake the rigors of self-examination in the next steps.

8

Clean House:
Look Deeply Within

Step Four: "Made a searching and fearless moral inventory of ourselves."

Step Five: "Admitted to God, to ourselves, and to another human being the exact nature of our wrongs."

"Anger is simply our way of reminding ourselves that we have a problem that needs attention."

—Frederic Luskin

At 40 years old, I faced a turning point in my life. I had entered the seminary at 13 and had been ordained a Catholic priest for 14 years. My whole life had revolved around serving in the Church. Then, I fell in love. My familiar life was turned upside down. I had a decision to make, either to remain a celibate priest or leave to get married. I felt lost, adrift on a stormy sea with no land in sight.

Fortunately, because I had been raised Catholic and developed the practice of a regular examination of conscience and confession, I had a life raft. However, the conventional religious routine seemed small and inadequate at the time. I prayed for God's guidance, consulted with my spiritual advisor, and began therapy. For three years I probed my desires and motivation with my therapist. It was a sort of intense personal inventory and confession. Aware of my capacity for self-deception, I needed a companion on this perilous journey. I asked myself many questions. Was I acting out of lust or love? Although I committed to the priesthood, had I really made a mature decision for celibacy? What were my deepest desires and commitments? What did God want of me? Finally, after three years of soul-searching, I felt free enough to make a decision. I left the active ministry and married. I became a psychologist to help others negotiate the transitions in their lives.

In your life's journey of facing your anger, the Steps invite you to a third leap of faith. The anger you so desperately want to escape is not your real problem. It is only a symptom of it. You must look deeply within yourself, search your soul, to discover what underlying character defects keep you stuck in your anger addiction. You must lean into and learn the message of your anger. What is your hostile reacting telling you about yourself? Your anger reveals what you cling to, what you imagine you need for happiness and loss of fear. Only dispelling these hidden illusions will set you free.

Steps four and five bring you to the brink of this leap of faith into self-discovery. You need to take a moral inventory and then tell another what you learned about yourself. Your house cleaning will continue with steps six and seven, when you dig deeper to discover the roots of your faults and ask God to remove them. The practice of these steps follows a well-worn path towards personal transformation. Christians call it "the purgative way," a here-and-now purgatory. Muslims call it "cleaning the mirror," so you can better reflect God's glory. The *Tao Te Ching*, written 25 centuries ago, describes the steps of the path:

> When he makes a mistake he realizes it.
> Having realized it, he admits it.
> Having admitted it, he corrects it (61).

Obstacles to Soul-Searching: The Blame Game

Realizing your mistakes requires humility, which is truth. Humility means seeing yourself as you really are, not as you wish to be. This honest self-examination involves walking a difficult middle path between denial and self-loathing. The biggest obstacle to this soul-searching is pride, your desire to be perfect. That perfectionism represents a secret desire to be God, all-knowing and all-powerful. The Steps/Traditions book warns: "This perverse soul-sickness is not pleasant to look at. Instincts on rampage balk at investigation" (p. 44).

Pride shows itself in two opposing ways: as ego-inflation and ego-deflation. You think of yourself as more or less than you really are. The excessive anger expresses itself as either a relentless blame of others or yourself. In either case, the blame distracts you from taking full responsibility for yourself.

Theodore, self-righteously angry:

> *"I admit that I have a temper. I'm an honest person and speak my mind. I tell it like it is, without sugar-coating it. I think people appreciate my honesty, though they may not like how blunt I can be. Frankly, some people can really make me mad when they behave so stupidly. I blow up, but then it's over. I get it off my chest and it's done. It's not like I hang on to the anger like some people I know. My temper is really no big deal."*

Some see themselves as bigger than their faults and overlook them. You may develop an inflated self-image and see yourself above reproach. In your mind, you transform your weaknesses, even your anger, into strengths. You imagine that others are responsible for your temper outbursts and blame them for your emotional reactions. As the Steps/Traditions book states, "Anger and hurt pride might be the smoke screen under which we were hiding some of our defects while we blamed others for them" (p. 59).

However, the charade cannot last forever. Sooner or later you will be exposed. Your anger will inevitably create some crisis, which can be a blessing if it leads you on the path to honest self-exploration. Will Rogers remarked, "People who fly into a rage always make a bad landing." Remember also that others may push your buttons, but they did not install them.

Tamara, swamped with self-loathing:

"I can't do anything right. Last week I went for a job interview. I worried about it for a week beforehand. I just knew I would do something to sabotage it. There was no way that they would like me. Frankly, I was shocked when they called me for the interview. Sure enough, during the interview I became tongue tied. I fumbled on the simplest questions. I knew the answers, but could not speak clearly. I'm still waiting to hear their decision. I'm sure not counting on being hired."

Others view their faults as larger than themselves. You may only see your weaknesses and ignore your strengths. That is really pride in reverse. You measure yourself against impossible standards of perfection and inevitably fail. You then become obsessed with your imperfections and lose a balanced view of yourself. As the Steps/Traditions book relates, "Too much guilt and remorse might cause us to dramatize and exaggerate our shortcomings" (p. 59).

Whether you direct your anger outward in blaming others or inward against yourself, you are stuck in a negative self-centeredness. No one lives up to your unrealistic standards. You make yourself the judge, constantly evaluating yourself and others. You believe the world must dance to your tune, according to your expectations. Being lost in the thoughts of how you think the world should be prevents you from seeing clearly. It interferes with an honest moral inventory. But there is a way out, by trusting your Higher Power.

The Power of Discernment

Working steps two and three, you began to trust in your Higher Power, by whatever name you gave it. It is your higher consciousness, through which you can stand back and observe the flow of your thoughts, feelings, and behaviors. If you pay close attention, you will observe that your consciousness is energized by anger in the face of injustice and falsehood. You have a natural intolerance of wrongdoing and deceit. You are better than some of your behaviors. In religious traditions, it is called "conscience."

The Higher Power of your consciousness is the white fire of awareness. It enlightens, sears, and purifies. That fiery conscience exposes false illusions and destroys them. It is like the sunlight on a misty morning. As the sun rises, you see the fog settling near the ground. As the day warms up, the fog dissipates. The heat and light from the sun sustain life and clean up the earth. Consciousness can also be likened to a fiery sword of discernment. Used wisely, it is a valuable weapon of defense against the onslaught of wickedness, both within and without. It can cut through deceit and destroy it.

Your Higher Power, if you come to trust it, enables you to exercise critical judgment in the face of confusion. When reactions arise, you can ask yourself, "Does this really make sense?" For example, when someone criticizes you, you can evaluate its merit. Then, you have a choice. You can put faith in your automatic reaction, which is often fed by illusions, or you can trust your innate wisdom. Your anger, when used well, possesses the wisdom of clarity. It can cut through all the crap and lead you to your truth, becoming a tool for personal change.

How can you use your power of discernment in taking your moral inventory? Spend time in quiet reflection. Take an honest look at your life. Stand back in your mind and become an observer. What do you see? You may even write what you observe in the flow of your sensations, feelings, and thoughts in a journal. There are four steps to this self-examination of your anger: recognize, accept, investigate, and disillusion.

1) Anger Recognition

Surprisingly, it is not always easy to recognize your anger. It can be subtle, cunning, and baffling, like any addiction. Thich Nhat Hanh, the Buddhist monk from Vietnam, suggested that we embrace our anger as a crying baby (1). When a baby cries, we know that something is wrong. However, the infant cannot put words to its discomfort. We are left guessing, so we hug the baby lovingly and observe it closely to discover the problem. When crying out in anger, hold yourself lovingly and pay close attention to several areas: your physical sensations, feelings, thoughts, words, and actions.

From my personal experience, I buried my anger so deeply that I was mostly unaware of it. It has been a long process for me to come into touch with its power and learn to use it wisely. My wife, who knows me well, would often point it out to me when she noticed my anger. "You seem tense. Is something wrong? Are you upset (angry) about something?" she would ask. She observed closely my facial expressions, mannerisms, and tense posture to identify my angry reactions.

Your physical sensations reveal your anger first because, like your animal ancestors, your body is preparing for battle. Notice the tension you feel, particularly in your shoulders and neck. Your facial expression may become contorted and reddened. Your heart rate may increase, and you may perspire, feeling hot under the collar. You may tremble with rage or have butterflies in your stomach. One patient told me he felt a "click" in his face when anger arose. Pay attention to your own unique signs.

Feeling states present another indication of anger. As mentioned previously, when you tend to stuff your anger, you have difficulty identifying it. This is characteristic of the passive-aggressive style. Internalized anger may show itself in a depressed mood, irritability, or increased anxiety. You may brood and feel frustrated or out-of-sorts. You may feel grumpy, irritated, or disgusted. The intense feelings of anger expressed in fury, bitterness, or temper outbursts are easy to identify, but internalized anger plays out in equally destructive ways. Know your own anger style and pay attention to the subtle shifts of mood.

Excessive anger is a disease of the mind. It is revealed in a pattern of negative thinking. When you are angry, you feel wronged or frustrated in the pursuit of a goal. You see others as the enemy or obstacles to what you want. You imagine malevolent intentions and desire to retaliate. Thoughts of being offended, revenge, and resentment fill your mind.

Hostile thoughts can be more subtle and not seen for the aggressiveness they express. One man came to see me complaining of back pain. He said, "I've been to so many doctors to find out what is causing the pain. They tell me there is no medical reason for me hurting so much. I have to believe that my emotions are causing it. I read several books that suggest suppressed anger causes tension in the back which results in pain, but I don't see myself as angry."

I invited him to pay close attention to the thoughts that ran through his mind. Initially, he had trouble identifying his thoughts. After some practice, he noticed, "I tend to judge other people and can be very critical. I don't say anything, but the thoughts are there. I also noticed that I'm self-conscious about other people judging me."

I explained, "The angry mind focuses on the negative, on what is being taken away from you or how you are not measuring up. Harsh criticisms, being judgmental of yourself and others, are definite signs of anger."

Words often follow thoughts. It is said, "The pen is mightier than the sword." I add, "The tongue also is mightier than the sword." Our words are powerful. What we say about ourselves and others creates our reality. As much harm can be done with words as with deeds. Evil speech can undermine trust and destroy relationships. Notice the many ways you may use aggressive language. You may gossip, slander, or harshly criticize others. You may lie, complain, or make sarcastic comments. Name-calling and profanity express aggression. Also pay attention to your self-talk. You can be as brutal with yourself as you are with others, and destroy yourself in the process.

You are likely more attuned to the many ways you express anger in action. These deeds are most visible. Courts punish observable, harmful actions. You most likely grew up learning the Ten Commandments that focus on what not to do, identifying clearly harmful behavior. Notice also the aggression expressed in neglecting yourself and others, which can be passive-aggressive. Not attending to your own physical, emotional, and spiritual needs does violence to yourself. Withdrawing emotionally from loved ones can be hostile. Not helping others in need when you are able can be an affront against them.

2) Anger Acceptance

You naturally hold a crying infant with love, not impatience. Likewise, nurturing your anger requires, in addition to recognizing the pain, accepting it lovingly. Rejecting your anger condition is a hostile act. It does not remove it. The impatience with yourself only reinforces your anger. One woman, who was going through a painful divorce, told me during a session, "You must be impatient with me because I'm not getting better. I keep making the same complaints every week. You must be tired of me."

"What makes you think I'm tired of you? Are you impatient with yourself?" I asked.

"I guess I am. I also don't want to be a burden to you," she admitted.

"Perhaps you think I will dismiss you as you are dismissing yourself," I interpreted.

Healing can happen only if you come to love yourself as you are, not as you wish you would be. The Buddha, the first and perhaps greatest scientist of the mind, said, "Hate never dispelled hate. Only love dispels hate. This is the law, ancient and inexhaustible." Impatience with oneself is a form of violence that escalates. Only loving acceptance of yourself can break the cycle.

3) Anger Investigation

Love makes you want to understand your child and relieve its suffering. After recognizing and accepting your anger, you can begin to investigate it. Your angry reaction is at the surface of your life. You must unpeel the onion to reveal the various layers of desire, fear, and pain that underlie it. When patients come to me telling me about their anger, I ask them, "What are you angry about?" I invite them to begin investigating their own emotional reaction. They often come up with a list of complaints about how others, their situation, or even life itself has wronged them. They may believe that these circumstances caused them to be angry. I then point out, "You give a lot of power to things outside yourself to affect your emotional wellbeing. Does your anger change anything? Look what it does to you." An AA adage states, "Nurturing anger is like consuming rat poison and expecting the rat to die."

I invite my patients to look more deeply into the nature of their anger. I encourage them to see the seeds of anger within themselves, rather than outside themselves. I tell them, "Your anger comes from within you. The event does not cause it. It's how you react to what's happening to you. That's really good news because you can change yourself, but not many circumstances in your life."

Like any addiction, anger is a self-centered reaction to not getting what you want. Some instinctual need has dominated your life, such as the normal desire for security and safety, power and control, self-esteem and affection. The Steps/Traditions book observed, "Powerfully, blindly, and many times subtly, they (these instincts) drive us, dominate us, and insist upon ruling our lives" (p.42). Your life becomes out of balance in the blind pursuit of some desire you believe essential for your happiness. Fear then enters the picture. You become terrified of losing what you want so desperately.

When you are in the grip of anger, stop to observe the thoughts running through your mind. Ask yourself the following questions:

- What event triggered my angry reaction?

- What desire or need was not being met?

- What is being threatened?

- What are my expectations about myself and others?

- How am I feeling powerless?

- What does my anger say about me?

Your anger reveals your sensitivity, what you hold dear. The following are some typical sticking points you may discover as you peel away the skins of your anger. An initial angry reaction may be normal. However, when your anger is excessive or prolonged, it indicates that you are hanging on to a desire too tightly.

"I got pissed when my friend insulted me." If you dwell on insults, you may have a fragile self-esteem, which you believe you must protect with your anger. Any criticism may assault your need to see yourself as perfect, always right, or in control.

"I lost it when my girlfriend left me." You may naturally grieve the loss of an important relationship. However, if you become obsessed about the lost love, you may be addicted to being loved, believing that only a relationship can make you happy.

"I stewed about it when someone else was promoted at work." You may value status and prestige, how you appear in others' eyes. Your envy may indicate a craving for approval from others.

"I was furious when that driver narrowly missed hitting me." You react because you fear physical harm. However, much road rage disguises a sense of vulnerability in other areas of life.

"I had a fit when my wife manipulated me into buying that expensive house." You may value power and control to the point that your sense of wellbeing depends on it.

"I went ballistic when my coworker stole my client." You may be driven by success and feel violated when someone unfairly steals it. You resent the injustice and loss of control.

4) Anger Disillusion

Your angry reactions may be so engrained that you tell yourself, "That's just who I am. I cannot change." However, as you investigate your anger with your discerning mind, you discover that your reactions are not as solid as you imagine. Your anger may seem to possess you completely for the moment, but as you calm down and observe yourself, you note that the thoughts and feelings pass, like morning mist. The terrible threats you imagine do not touch the core of who you are as a person. In fact, the dangers are often exaggerated or even a figment of your imagination. You imagine that your happiness depends on being loved, being successful, having approval, and so forth, but you discover that these beliefs are all an illusion.

I invite my patients to notice the illusory quality of their reactions. One patient complained, "I was so upset when my boss corrected me that I could not sleep. I knew my job wasn't threatened, yet I kept going over it in my mind."

"What bothered you so much about it?" I asked.

"It was just so unfair," he said.

"Then why not just ignore it?" I suggested.

"Well, it hurt my feelings," he explained.

"What feelings?" I enquired.

"I guess my pride was hurt," he replied.

"Show me your pride. Where is it?" I responded, looking around the room. I encouraged him to see that his reaction was merely a passing thought in his mind that had no more reality than he gave it.

The recovery of your true self occurs as you progressively give up your illusions and empty expectations about how you and your life should be. You gain a sense of who you really are beneath the chaos and drama of the hostile reacting. As you surrender these illusions, you begin to live in truth. You begin to appreciate the depth of the mystery of who you are.

Look to Others

Self-reflection may not be enough to plumb your depths. Humbly aware of your limits, you do not need to rely on yourself alone for your moral inventory. You can learn from others. Relationships reveal problems and who you really are.

There is a popular myth in our culture that relationships solve problems. For example, if you are lonely, need to be loved, or want companionship, the solution is to become involved with someone. However, over time, when these needs are not met in the ways you expect, disillusionment sets in. Then, you imagine that your relationship is causing your unhappiness. The solution is to discard that relationship and begin again with another person, someone you imagine is the right person. Eventually, you are dissatisfied with what that person gives you. The cycle of misery continues until you recognize the value of the relationship to increase your self-awareness and propel you on your path of personal transformation.

Two kinds of people are particularly helpful on your path: your critics and your enemies. First, welcome criticism and see your critics as teachers. The *Tao Te Ching* states, "(A great man) considers those who point out his faults as his most benevolent teachers" (61). You have blind spots, like everybody else. Those who criticize you can give you valuable feedback. They can give you a different perspective on yourself, letting you know how you come across to others. You might be surprised at what you hear if you are open.

Can criticism and correction really hurt you? Always evaluate what others say about you, weighing its truthfulness. Take what helps, and discard the rest. No one likes criticism. You may secretly yearn to be perfect. The criticism of others has power to disturb you to the extent that it echoes what you are already telling yourself. Your own inner critic is harsher than anything or anyone else.

Secondly, see your enemy as your shadow. "(A great man) thinks of his enemy as the shadow that he himself casts," the *Tao Te Ching* (61) observes. When I meet with a patient who complains about someone in their lives, I encourage them to tell me in detail what they do not like about that person. One patient told me, "I can't stand my boss. He's the most two-faced man I ever met. He makes so many promises that he never keeps that I don't believe anything he says."

I then asked, "Can you identify with anything you don't like about your boss?"

My patient had a stunned look on his face. He was having an affair.

To avoid looking honestly at yourself, you may turn your attention to the faults of others. You see the splinter in their eye, not the plank in your own. I encourage you to pay close attention to what you dislike in others, to what drives you crazy about them. Notice their annoying habits. However, instead of condemning them, ask yourself honestly if you can identify with any of those irritating behaviors. If you are honest with yourself, you will discover that what you hate in others, you despise and disown in yourself. In other words, "If you spot it, you got it," or as we said when I was a child, "It takes one to know one."

Confess to Another

A third resource to help you know yourself is in admitting your faults to someone you trust, such as a close friend, your spouse, your minister or priest, or a therapist. It takes a great deal of courage to expose your shadow, what you do not like about yourself. Intimacy entails risk. Yet the benefits are considerable. What will you receive in return for taking the risk?

1) Overcome Isolation

The armor of anger insulates and isolates. Your anger pushes people away until, eventually, you are alone. The fifth step encourages you to move out of your isolation to connect with another. You seek support in bearing the burden of your faults. As the AA saying goes, "If you share your pain, you cut it in half; if you don't, you double it." In taking the risk to disclose yourself, you confront directly your tendency to mistrust others. Acting against your urge to attack or withdraw, you gain confidence to rebuild broken relationships.

The benefit of reaching out to others is contentment. The cost of staying isolated is loneliness.

2) Receive Acceptance

Your angry mind judges harshly and rejects others and yourself. You see enemies everywhere. How can you free yourself from your mental habits of judgment and rejection? Telling another about your wrongdoing brings you face-to-face with your self-defeating habits. It presents an opportunity to unmask them. Your humble, honest, courageous self-exposure inevitably invites a favorable response from your listener. Instead of the expected rejection, you receive an open-hearted acceptance. The surprise may shock you into awareness that forgiveness is available for even the most grievous faults. One patient told me, "I was so nervous reading my inventory to my sponsor I could hardly talk. When it was over, he gave me a big hug, and I realized it was all no big deal." As if by some miracle, feeling forgiven opens your heart to forgive yourself.

The benefit of risking rejection is surprising acceptance. The cost of holding back is remaining the slave of your rejecting mind.

3) Experience Humility

"The road to disappointment and resentment is paved by expectations," an AA saying states. Unfulfilled expectations regarding yourself and others fuel your anger. Some of these expectations may be unrealistic and disguise a hidden pride. You take a major step toward humbly accepting yourself by admitting your faults to another. You come out of hiding behind the mask of how you imagine life should be. You no longer have to be an actor in the drama of your life. What you risk in telling the truth about yourself is losing your pride and your shame. What a relief there is in giving up the burden of maintaining the pretense of a false self. You can relax into being an ordinary human being, like everyone else, with strengths and weaknesses.

The benefit of risking humiliation is the letting go of your pride. The cost of not taking the chance is the relentless drive to continue proving how good and right you are.

4) Confront Self-Deception

Drugged by anger, your mind is in a fog. You cannot think clearly or choose wisely. When you take the fifth step, you invite another to bear witness to your sorrow and the suffering you cause yourself and others by your self-centered anger. You expose the pride, greed, envy, and other faults that underlie your hostile mood. Furthermore, your honest self-disclosure also invites honest feedback from your listener. You gain another perspective on your behavior. Perhaps you exaggerated or minimized your faults, or did not look deeply enough into them. You may even ask your listener for advice and counsel, which can give you helpful direction on the perilous road of recovery. You do not have to travel alone.

The benefit of letting another know you is the gift of honesty. The cost of keeping yourself hidden is a life of illusion.

5) Show Your Strength

Your anger may compensate for a sense of powerlessness. By admitting your weaknesses to another, you actually show your strengths. It takes honesty, humility, and courage to expose yourself. You can acknowledge your faults only after taking an honest look at yourself. Refusing to hide behind your façade of superiority or inferiority requires humility. Risking the judgment and rejection of another confronts your craving for approval. That takes courage. Displaying your strengths gives you and another person a glimpse of the personal goodness and abundance that lies behind your angry face.

The benefit of admitting your weaknesses is appreciating your hidden strengths. The cost of secretly dwelling on your faults is self-hatred.

6) Sense of God's Presence

Anger colors your world. You may see the universe as hostile, others as enemies, and God as a harsh Judge. Your hostile attitude drains you of hope and energy. Meeting another in honest dialogue can open up your heart and mind.

Relationships generate energy greater than the energy of each individual separately. That is precisely the reason alcoholics formed a fellowship for mutual healing. Exposing your weaknesses to others and experiencing their acceptance releases a hidden power. The interaction releases the power of love. As Freud observed, healing comes through the love expressed in the relationship with another.

Imagine two individuals in a relationship as two intersecting circles. Part of each circle is separate, while another area is shared. The meeting of the two circles creates a third oblong shape. The shared area has a relational energy, created by the contribution of each individual. That energy is greater than the sum total of the energy of each individual. You experience in heart-felt intimacy a Power greater than yourself that comes from you, but is beyond you. That Power is life-giving.

Those of a religious temperament experience it as a sacred presence. As Jesus teaches, "Where two or three are gathered in my name, I am in their midst." John, the beloved disciple, wrote, "God is love. Whoever lives in love lives in God and God in him."

The benefit of meeting with others is the opportunity to encounter a Power greater than yourself. The cost of staying alone is a magnified feeling of powerlessness.

Paradox of Death and Life

As you work through steps four and five to clean house, you may become mortified by what you discover. You never realized the fearful self-centeredness that fueled your anger. You never noticed how you had regressed to a two year old, throwing a temper tantrum when you did not get what you wanted. Such awareness can be humiliating. It may even cause you to hate yourself.

The leap of faith in making a moral inventory challenges you with another paradox: "We die to live." Instead of hating your life as it is, it invites you to embrace it with love, even with all the pain you cause yourself and others by your anger. Your pain can be the way to new life. Jesus said, "I solemnly assure you, unless the grain of wheat falls to the earth and dies, it remains just a grain of wheat. But if it dies, it produces much fruit"(John 12:24). How can the anger you both love and hate bring you new life?

Your anger addiction can be a gift if it leads you to look more deeply into your life and ask, "What needs to die in me? What can come to life?" In your recovery, the unhealthy habits of the old self die through a gradual process of recognizing them, seeing their emptiness, and letting them go. Your clinging to the desire for power and control, safety and security, affection and self-esteem keeps you stuck and enslaves you. The white heat of awareness burns away your attachment to your vices and sets you free to be your true self.

Letting the seeds of selfishness die allows a new life to flower. What does that life look like? Freed from the illusion that satisfying your self-centered desires will bring you lasting happiness, your natural self can emerge. You are open to discover and live in truth and love. Instead of futilely trying to play God, you can be God-like in the way you live. In other words, you are free to love wholeheartedly, without reservation. As the Sufi poet Hafiz wrote, "We are people who need to love, because Love is the soul's life. Love is simply creation's greatest joy."

Practice: Loving-Kindness

Anger often hides a buried fear. An AA slogan states, "Anger is but a word for fear." A traditional Eastern practice to uproot fear is called *metta*, or loving-kindness (2). According to legend, it originated when a group of frightened monks approached the Buddha for help. They were being sent into the forest to meditate, but their fear and sense of helplessness stopped them. They heard stories about rampaging elephants, poisonous snakes, and ferocious tigers attacking people. As an antidote to their fear, the Buddha taught them the following practice of loving-kindness. It is noteworthy that he did not tell them to stay out of the forest or offer them physical protection. He approached their fear and dread as an affair of the mind and proposed a practice of mind training.

The practice is deceptively simple and powerful, engaging an unseen power within you:

1) Sit comfortably in a quiet place. Close your eyes and focus on the rhythm of your breath. Breathe deeply from your abdomen and allow the muscles of your body to relax. Sense the warmth of your breath radiating into your tense muscles, loosening the knots.

2) Once relaxed, consider for a moment where you are in life. Allow yourself to feel the stress, turmoil, and confusion. If you are preoccupied with your fault-finding expedition, feel deeply the guilt, shame, and disappointment in yourself.

3) Then select and focus your attention on phrases that address the pain and turmoil you feel in the moment. Express them as heart-felt wishes for yourself. For example, say to yourself: "May I be happy." "May I be free from anger and sorrow." "May I feel content with my life." "May I be kind and loving." "May I be patient with myself." "May I forgive myself." Add whatever wishes best express your deepest desires in the moment.

4) Repeat three or four phrases to yourself for a period of time. Repeat the phrases slowly and thoughtfully for about ten minutes. Coordinate the repetition of the phrases with the rise and fall of your breathing. Allow the words to sink into your mind and body.

This exercise fosters an attitude of loving-kindness toward yourself. It is the perfect antidote to fear, anger, and self-hatred. You can extend loving-kindness wishes to others in your life, radiating out towards your loved ones, towards anyone you encounter, towards those who harmed you, and towards the entire world.

Cleaning house involves you in a grieving process. You consider what to keep and what to throw away. You may surprise yourself with how much you love your faults and resist giving them up. As your self-examination continues in the next steps, you consider the cost and benefit of hanging on to them. Your hope for new life sustains you in this challenging task.

9

Clean House:
Digging Deeper

Step Six: "Were entirely ready to have God remove all these defects of character."

Step Seven: "Humbly asked Him (God) to remove our shortcomings."

*"Because we are in love with our vices, we uphold them
and prefer to make excuses for them rather than shake them off."*

—Seneca

"Life must be remembered backward, but lived forward," Soren Kierkegaard, the existentialist philosopher, observed. Looking backward in my therapy, I realized that I found a place of refuge from my chaotic childhood with alcoholic parents in my role as "the perfect child." Nearly all good Catholic families in the 1950s wanted one of their children to become a priest or nun. It was a selfless offering to God and a badge of honor for the family. I fulfilled their dream. In the fourth grade I became an altar boy, learned the Latin prayers, and practiced celebrating Mass at an altar in the basement. The fantasy of dedicating my life to God like the parish priest I admired gave me a sense of security and purpose.

From being the "perfect child," I aspired to be the "perfect priest." I always kept myself under strict control and never displayed any anger—at least outwardly. I fulfilled my duties, dedicated myself to my parishioners, and was respected and even loved by them. I took pride in my role and work. What I did not allow myself or others to know was the secret rage inside. It leaked inward in the excessive demands I made on myself in fulfilling my duties. It seeped out in my sense of arrogance and righteousness, hidden behind a meek façade. Internally, my mind was judgmental. I knew clearly what was right and wrong and became an obedient servant of the Church.

My decision to leave the active ministry was a humbling experience that brought me face-to-face with myself. It exposed my strength, but also my hidden motivations that cried out to be purified. There was little doubt about how much house cleaning I had yet to do.

House cleaning becomes more thorough with steps six and seven. You engage in deep cleaning, uncovering the roots of your anger. Patterns learned from childhood and enforced by the culture become evident. In your efforts to become "entirely ready" to remove "all your character defects," you encounter your inner resistance. You discover how much you love your faults, because you derive some benefit from them. As the Steps/Traditions book states, "Even the best of us will discover to our dismay that there is always a sticking point, a point at which we say, 'No, I can't give this up yet.' And we shall tread on even more dangerous ground when we cry, 'This I will never give up!'" (p. 66).

Admitting our love of our imperfections can be a humbling experience. In step one, you acknowledged your powerlessness over your anger. Now you face your powerlessness to untangle the knot of self-centered thoughts and feelings that give rise to your aggressiveness. Craving for control feeds your anger. Your recovery will depend on your willingness to surrender your pride and desire for control. That can be daunting. It can cause you to procrastinate on the path. One wisdom teacher warned, "Avoid the spiritual path. It's one humiliation after another."

You tell yourself, "I hate my anger and all the pain it causes me and those I love. I hate my imperfections. They only make me miserable. Then why am I so stuck, unwilling to change?"

Ghosts in the Basement

You are stuck because you are still living in the familiar past, fearful of the unknown future. "The past is not dead, it is not even past," William Faulkner observed. It still haunts you. What you learned in childhood shapes your emotional reacting, thinking, and behaving. You act as an adult from a template your parents and society programmed into you without your permission, and you do not even know it is happening. The ghosts hide in your unconscious mind.

You were born with a bundle of needs, completely dependent on your parents to satisfy them. Undoubtedly, your parents responded the best they could, but no one has perfect parents. Any needs that were not adequately fulfilled, like the need for security, control, or affection, did not disappear. Instead, they continued to cry out for attention (1).

In your wondrous resourcefulness as a growing child, you found ways of satisfying these basic needs. To feel safe and secure in your world, you may have learned to cling to loved ones or withdraw into your own world. You learned ways of gaining power and control over your life, perhaps through defiant rebellion or compliance with powerful adults. You sought ways to meet your needs for affection and self-esteem through interacting with others and pursuing your goals. Lacking a developed self-consciousness, you spontaneously pursued the satisfaction of your instinctual needs in order to survive. At an early age, you began to develop your own emotional programs to seek happiness and avoid suffering.

These emotional programs for happiness began to take shape before the birth of conscious awareness. You did not freely choose your unique path to happiness. You merely responded to the urgency of these instinctual needs in the circumstances of your family.

If you were raised in a good enough environment, these needs were satisfied in a spontaneous, natural, and balanced way. However, if you experienced some deprivation of any of these needs, you pursued what was lacking with emotional intensity, causing a lack of balance in your life. The need for security, power, or affection may have taken on an exaggerated importance and become an unconscious preoccupation.

As a child, you naturally compensate for what is missing in your life. Resentment towards your caregivers for not giving you what you needed may grow and be suppressed. Your anger, if acknowledged and expressed, would endanger the connection you need from them for survival.

The emotional programs for happiness, unconsciously pursued, shape your interests as you grow into adulthood. You may become fixated on the pursuit of security, power, or affection to the exclusion of other values. These pursuits may assume an addictive quality in their excessiveness and repetitiveness, and in your powerlessness to overcome. You may even begin to find your identity in the blind pursuit of these needs, believing they are essential for your happiness.

Furthermore, the culture may reinforce these messages regarding the pursuit of happiness. The American culture promises happiness through the acquisition of three Ps: possession, power, and prestige. It proclaims: "You can find security in having money, comforts, and possessions; more is better." "Never show your weaknesses. You will be exploited. People admire the strong and powerful." "Always strive to be the best and never settle; that is the path to status and prestige." The culture promotes high expectations in chasing these goals.

Anger arises when these needs are not being met. Your wellbeing is threatened. Your anger also expresses what you value most and fear losing.

Getting Ready, Becoming Unstuck

How can you begin to loosen the grip of these childhood desires and fears? By exploring their roots in childhood and making them more conscious. You may have learned from your parents how to manage your anger, how to think negatively and not positively, and how to imagine yourself.

Whenever I meet with patients, I invite them to tell me their stories. They tell me about what is bothering them and who they are. As the therapy progresses, their self-narratives unfold. Together, we explore the meaning of their lives and the many ways they think about themselves. I tell them, "That's an interesting way to think about yourself. How did you learn to think that way?" We then explore childhood influences and consider alternative ways of thinking. For example, I met with a middle-aged couple, Linda and Ralph, who could not communicate without arguing. They acknowledged that any discussion became a power struggle. They felt clueless about how to manage their anger.

Linda complained, "I hate it when Ralph withdraws and refuses to talk. He just gives me the silent treatment after an argument, and nothing gets resolved. I know when he's angry and doesn't like something, but he doesn't speak up. It's so frustrating."

Ralph chimed in, after some encouragement, "I can't stand Linda's temper. When she raises her voice, I clam up and just want to run away."

I observed their differing anger styles, how Linda tended to be more expressive, while Ralph internalized more and became fearful. I asked them how they learned their ways of managing their anger.

Linda spoke up first. "My parents divorced when I was young. My mother was a strong-willed woman who raised us five children on her own. She was often away at work. I learned at an early age that I had to speak up and fight to get what I wanted."

Ralph said, "I was afraid of my father who had a terrible temper. I learned at a young age that I had to shut up to survive."

They immediately saw the connection between their childhood reacting and their interactions as adults. I pointed out, "You are not that helpless child anymore. Now you are an adult with resources you never had then. You can choose to act differently." I encouraged them simply to be aware of their reacting and affirmed their freedom to respond any way they saw fit. Edmund Burke warned, "Those who do not learn from their past are condemned to repeat it."

You can ask yourself about how anger was managed when you were a child:

- What is your current anger style and where did you learn it?

- How did each of your parents express their anger? What were their anger styles? Did they yell, blame, argue, give the silent treatment, or become violent?

- What messages did you receive about expressing your anger? Were you punished or rewarded?

- Were you encouraged to express your feelings? Was your voice heard?

Here Comes the Judge

In addition to your anger styles, you learned from your parents how to think and engage your world. When patients with anger problems come to me and speak about some incident in which they lost their temper or held a grudge, I ask, "What were you saying to yourself when you were so angry?"

"I don't know. I was just angry," they often respond.

I explain, "Feelings last 90 seconds. They come and they go. What intensifies any feeling and makes it last are the stories you tell yourself." I invite them to pay attention to the thoughts that accompany their feelings.

Almost without exception, negative, judgmental ideas flood their minds when angry. They believe they were wronged. Someone did not act the way they expected, and they took offense. They dwell on the injustice of that person's behavior, imagining they tried to hurt them on purpose. Their minds then shift to how they can retaliate. They feel entitled to their anger and striking back. Thoughts of revenge may occupy them as they ruminate about the hurt. They fantasize that they are restoring the balance of power. The other person has become the enemy.

Anger begins and grows from a thought. In fact, anger can be viewed as feeling plus judgment. The valence of the thought, whether positive or negative, shapes the neutral energy of anger. It can become aggression with negative, critical judgment, which is rejecting, or it can be discernment, with wise judgment. The tiny seed of anger can grow until it flowers into violent behavior. The Hindu sage, Maharaj, observed the progression, "Between desire and fear, anger arises; with anger, hatred; and with hatred, passion for destruction. War is hatred in action, organized and equipped with all the instruments of death" (1). If you want to end war, then make peace in your heart and avoid negative judgment.

When my patients become attuned to the flow of their thoughts, they tell me about how judgmental they were of the person who harmed them. I ask, "Who is our only judge?"

"That would be God," they say.

"Then whose role are you taking when you act as judge?" I enquire.

"I suppose I'm playing God," they respond.

I then ask, "What standards, what expectations, are you using to judge others and yourself?"

They often present a list of "shoulds." I then enquire, "Where did that list come from? How did you learn to think that way?" That leads us into a journey back into their childhoods.

Cecilia, an angry, depressed woman:

"I could never please my mother. Anything I did wasn't good enough. I tried so hard to please her and always felt like a failure. I blamed myself. Even today I hear her voice in my head, even though she has been dead for 20 years. Whenever I'm doing anything, I hear her say, 'You're not doing it right. What's the matter with you? Are you stupid?' So I question myself constantly."

Ask yourself what messages you received from childhood:

- How negative and critical were your parents?
- What were their expectations of you? Were they realistic?
- Did you feel like you could never please them?
- Did you blame yourself? Did you become excessively demanding of others?

Storytelling

A third way parents influence us is through identification. We come to know ourselves by knowing them. Our interactions with them provide the memories and images that shape our self-identity.

Patients come to tell me their stories of pain and sorrow. They want relief from their suffering. I listen carefully with my third ear, my innate intuition, to understand the source and cause of their pain. They relate events when they felt mistreated as adults, which often mirror experiences of abuse or neglect as children. What emerges in the discussion is the outline of a self-image they inherited by identifying with one or both of their parents. "The apple doesn't fall far from the tree," they say when I point out the similarity with their parents.

No one survives childhood without being hurt in some way. Your needs were never perfectly met. The imprints of imperfect parenting remain. Of course, there are degrees of woundedness, from benign neglect to outright abuse. Your anger conceals a bundle of feelings from your early life: fear, shame, guilt, hurt, and sadness. However, if your anger is intense and uncontrollable, whether directed inward or outward, it is a sign that your childhood experience was toward the traumatic end of the spectrum and you anger covers over intense feelings.

The primary emotion of those deeply wounded is fear. Traumatized, you feel powerless in a threatening world. You grasp at whatever pleasure you can find and fight to protect it. Your anger gives you a sense of control over your life. It stands as a monument of protest against your mistreatment, but it also keeps you stuck in the past, in your misery. The Steps/Traditions book states, "The chief activator of our defects has been self-centered fear—primarily fear that we would lose something we already possessed or would fail to get something we demanded. Living on a basis of unsatisfied demands, we were in a state of continual disturbance and frustration" (2).

Three False Identities

To cope, you use your mind to make sense of your world. Memory and imagination produce a personal narrative. The pain and fear are expressed in stories you tell yourself and that shape your self-image. The stories solidify into a personality with definable characteristics. I have noticed three common patterns of story-telling among those most enraged. They identify themselves as victims, bullies, or caretakers.

Colleen, a fearful victim:

"I make the worst choices in men. All of them have been losers who treated me terribly. It happens over and over again, and I don't understand it. My current boyfriend doesn't work. He just sits around the house, drinks beer, and expects me to wait on him. He has a temper. When I don't do what he wants, he screams at me. I complain about him to my girlfriends all the time. They ask me why I put up with it. I guess I'm just afraid to be alone."

If you see yourself as a victim, you constantly tell yourself, "The world is a dangerous place; I can't protect myself." You live with a sense of helplessness in a threatening world. However, you feel so defenseless because you suppress your anger, which would energize you to fight back. Instead, you surrender your natural power, and your anxiety increases. As a victim, you unknowingly become passive aggressive. You complain and blame others for your misery, taking little responsibility for your own wellbeing. Your fear prevents you from standing up for yourself. You have a ready-made excuse for not living an active life.

Brian, a proud bully:

> *"I don't apologize that I stand up for myself and for what I believe is right. Some people call me pushy, but that's their problem. I won't let people push me around or take advantage of me. I admit that sometimes I have a temper when I don't get my way. Everyone knows what I think and what I'm not willing to tolerate. My father was a milk toast, and my mother bossed him around. I promised myself I would never be a weakling like my father."*

If you are a bully who freely expresses your anger in an aggressive way, you may justify it, saying, "I'm just standing up for myself." However, you may be blind to the damage your temper causes yourself and others. Like the victim, you see the world as a threatening place, with enemies around every corner. You fear being powerless. Unlike the victim, though, you assert yourself, sometimes in the extreme. You value power and control over your life. Our culture supports you in the aggressive pursuit of what you believe will make you happy while ignoring the cost to others.

Dorothy, the guilty caretaker:

> *"My father was a mean drunk. When he came home from work, he ordered all of us around. He used to beat our mother. I felt so sorry for her and wanted to help lighten her load. I'm the oldest of six children, so I guess I just naturally took over when mom wasn't available. She used to get depressed and stay in her room. I took care of the younger children, fixed dinner, and organized the cleaning of the house. Now, as an adult, everyone in the family comes to me for help and advice, and I'm always available."*

If you assume the role of caretaker or rescuer, you become attuned to the needs of those around you. However, you may become disconnected from yourself. Ironically, you imagine you know exactly what others need, but are clueless about what is best for you. Often, you neglect yourself and pay the price. Your need to be needed compels you to sacrifice yourself. The payoff is the admiration of others. However, what is hidden from yourself and others is your rage at all the responsibility dumped on you. Feeling guilty for your suppressed anger, you neglect yourself and try to make reparations by helping others. Your anger shows itself when those you aid do not express appreciation or criticize you for your intrusiveness.

Fantasy Scripts

The habit of storytelling to guide your life begins in early childhood. Your personal stories are shaped by the messages you receive from your parents and from society and stored in your memory. Their voices are ghostlike and godlike, roaming in your unconscious mind. They reflect your early emotional programming of how you learned to cope with life and find happiness. These childlike narratives become the lenses through which you view your experiences even as an adult. They are the scripts for the unfolding drama of your life.

Imagine that your mind is like a movie projector. From your memory and imagination, you create a movie of your life and project it on a screen for yourself and others to see. In your film, you are the main character, the hero, undergoing trials in pursuing happiness. If you suffer from anxiety, depression, or an anger sickness, your show is likely a horror movie. Many monsters block your way. Dark thoughts fill your mind and are projected outward on the blank screen. You cannot stop the projector. Showing images is only natural. However, a problem arises when you believe the movie is real and the monsters in your mind are real. Then, the illusion of a threatening world dominates your innate peace of mind.

How can you distinguish reality and fantasy within your mind's projections? Simply stop and observe the flow of thoughts, feelings, and images. Be mindful. Trust your wise mind of acceptance and discernment.

Ask yourself what experiences shaped your self-image:

- With which parent do you identify more?

- What qualities do you admire in your parents? What qualities do you want to avoid?

- What values did they emphasize in raising you? What behaviors did they teach you to avoid?

- What were their expectations of you?

Cost/Benefit Analysis of Your Self-Image

When my patients tell me their stories and label themselves, I ask, "What purpose do you think it could serve for you to think about yourself that way?" I invite them to engage in an analysis of the costs and benefits of their habitual way of thinking. I encourage them to involve their wise, rational mind in the work.

If you identify yourself with the "victim role," what are some advantages for you?

- You are acutely aware of your vulnerability and take steps to protect yourself.

- You are cautious in trusting and loyal when you find someone trustworthy.

- You can learn to assert yourself.

- Others may offer you sympathy and want to help.

But, what are some disadvantages of the victim role?

- You may indulge a sense of helplessness and not take action.

- You may blame others for your problems and not take responsibility.

- Others may try to exploit your weakness.

If you see yourself as a "bully," what are the possible benefits of thinking that way?

- You can rationalize your aggressive behavior.

- You can intimidate others to get your way.

- You may feel strong and powerful pushing others around.

But, what are the possible costs of this self-label?

- You fail to recognize the harm you cause yourself and others by your aggression.

- You alienate others and destroy relationships.

- Your self-esteem suffers as you continue to live the illusion of power.

If you label yourself a "caretaker," what do you gain?

- Your self-esteem increases as you help others.

- Others may benefit from your care.

- Others may admire you.

But, what do you lose?

- Neglecting yourself, your health may suffer.

- You may become angry at others exploiting you.

- You may not learn to set boundaries in relationships.

Through the power of awareness, you begin to loosen the grip of the character defects that underlie your anger. Your defects are rooted in childhood desires and fears, which are mostly unconscious. From your parents, you learned how to manage your anger, think negatively, and imagine yourself. To survive, you imitated them. Now you see more clearly the emptiness of the negative thinking and false self-identifications. They are simply thoughts, not facts. These fixed ideas interfere with your openness to reality. Ready to surrender your faults, you realize you cannot remove them through your own effort. You need a Power greater than yourself, so you humbly ask for God's help.

Humbly Asking

In the Christian tradition, Saint Paul presents a model of humbly asking. Paul was a passionate man. As a devout Jew, he persecuted the early followers of Jesus because he saw them as heretics. After his conversion, he dedicated his life to serving Jesus and spreading the Good News. Even as an apostle to the Gentiles, Paul remained a man of many passions that were often in conflict within him. He confessed, "I cannot even understand my own actions. I do not do what I want to do but what I hate...What a wretched man I am!" (3).

To resolve this painful inner conflict, Paul turned to prayer. He recounts, "...in order that I might not become conceited I was given a thorn in the flesh, an angel of Satan to beat me and keep me from getting proud. Three times I begged the Lord that this might leave me." His fervent prayer was answered in an unexpected way. "He (Jesus) said to me, 'My grace is enough for you, for in weakness power reaches perfection." And so I willingly boast of my weaknesses instead…for when I am powerless, it is then that I am strong" (II Cor. 12:7-10). God did not remove the thorn in his flesh as he asked. Instead, through accepting his weaknesses, Paul learned humility and discovered a hidden power within. He gained the power of accepting himself as he was.

In a similar way, working the Steps punctures your ego and brings you to humility. You face your inner conflicts and powerlessness to resolve them. The Steps/Traditions book expresses clearly this truth: "For us, the process of gaining a new perspective was unbeliev-ably painful. It was only by repeated humiliations that we were forced to learn something about humility. It was only at the end of a long road, marked by successive defeats and humiliations, and the final crushing of our self-sufficiency, that we began to feel humility as something more than a condition of groveling despair" (4).

What is the humility you are learning about? How does it help? The root word of hu-mility, "humus," gives a clue to its actual meaning. Humus means, "earth, ground." It is also the root word for "human." Being humble reminds you of the truth of who you really are as a human being. It gives you a balanced view of yourself. You see both the angels of your better nature and the demons of your baser desires. If you saw only the angels, you would become proud, conceited. If you knew only your demons, you would give up in shame and despair.

Humility enables you to accept your limitations and ask for help. You do not have com-plete control over your life. Facing your own stubbornness to surrender your shortcomings reminds you of your powerlessness. Humility invites you to empty yourself of your proud expectations of perfection. It encourages you to make space in your heart to be the right receiver, accepting wholeheartedly whatever comes. Like Saint Paul, you then can even boast of your weaknesses, release the hidden power within, and keep trying.

Transform, Not Remove

What do you pray for? You pray to remove your defects of character. However, your clear awareness reveals them as dirt on the surface of your psyche that can be wiped away. Your faults do not touch the core of who you are. Instead, they represent misguided at-tempts to cope with the pain and emptiness of your life. They are efforts to fill the hole in the soul. You seek happiness, but look in the wrong place. In reality, your hated vices are distortions of your strengths that need to be redirected to attain true happiness.

Consequently, the better strategy is to learn to transform, not remove, your shortcom-ings.

A traditional story illustrates the transforming strategy. Once upon a time, a poisoned tree grew in the middle of a village. All the elders gathered to decide what to do. One group saw only the danger in the tree's presence and recommended, "Let's cut it down before anyone is harmed." A second group countered, "Let's not hate it or fear it. After all, it's part of nature, which is good, and must be respected. We must have compassion for the tree because we share its nature. Let's build a fence around it so we will not get too close and get poisoned." The leader of the group listened to all the arguments and finally spoke up: "This poison tree is perfect, exactly what our village needs. Let's learn its secrets. Instead of destroying it or avoiding it, let's pick the poisoned fruit. Let's investigate it carefully and look for ways to use the poison as medicine to heal ourselves and others." Hearing that wisdom, all the elders stood up to affirm the decision.

The story suggests caution in trying to uproot your anger and underlying attachments too quickly. You may become impatient with yourself because your faults persist despite your best efforts. Trying to eliminate them may be an act of violence against yourself, which only intensifies your self-hatred.

A more useful approach is to lean into your feelings and learn their message. Observe and investigate closely the stream of sensations, feelings, thoughts, and stories to uncover their hidden treasure. Be open to the possibility that the seeds of virtue may sprout from your vices.

Paradox Of Doing And Not Doing

I often remind my patients, "Don't try to change yourself. Simply be yourself."

Often, they protest, "But I hate my anger and impatience. I want to change that about myself."

"Fighting your anger and impatience is a battle you cannot win. Hating your anger only keeps you stuck in the cycle of violence," I point out. In fact, an AA slogan observes, "What you resist persists."

"Then what can I do?" they ask.

"Simply be yourself," I repeat.

"But I don't know myself," they complain.

"That's the problem. Be quiet and pay attention. You'll get to know yourself. Then, you will know what to do," I explain. Action and contemplation work in tandem.

Steps six and seven clearly state the need for work and prayer, action and contemplation. You are instructed to "make yourself entirely ready" and "ask God" to remove your shortcomings. AA gives the general advice to "work the program" and "let go, and let God." There is a fine balance expressed in these two directives. If you believe that only your efforts count, you can become arrogant with success or despairing with defeat. If you believe that God does it all, you can slip into being a passive spectator in your life. Prayer or meditation prepares you for action, giving you confidence and direction. In turn, action, struggling to make a better life, brings you humbly to prayer.

Alcoholics Anonymous is not simply a self-help program. To make progress, you must admit your powerlessness over your faults and surrender to your Higher Power. This wisdom is expressed in the aphorism: "We let go to produce results." When you try to force change before you are ready, you stay stuck. The struggle indicates you are fighting the conflicting desires within your "Big Ego." There is no escape from that battle ground. However, when you are ready and cry for help, your progress is effortless. It flows naturally from your true self. The *Tao Te Ching* advocates a rhythm of both doing and not doing, letting events unfold naturally:

Less and less do you need to force things,
until finally you arrive at non-action.
When nothing is done,

nothing is left undone.
True mastery can be gained
by letting things go their own way.
It can't be gained by interfering (48).

Recovery from your anger addiction is like planting a garden and watching the flowers grow. It requires much effort to prepare the garden for growth. You cannot force flowers to bloom. They will not flourish unless you prepare the ground. You have to till the soil, plant seeds of good works, and pull the weeds of your shortcomings. Then the sun, rain, and warmth of your natural goodness allow the seeds to sprout and show forth their natural beauty. The hidden power of your true self works its wonders. You watch and wait, tending the garden as needed, and witness the miracle of new life.

Practice: Remaining Like a Log

Your anger can quickly ignite to become a firestorm, unless you learn to identify the smoldering tinder. The sooner you catch the rising anger, the easier it is to manage. An ancient Eastern text, *The Way of the Bodhisattva* (3), suggests a practice to stop, look, and listen to yourself before acting. The practice is called, "Remaining like a log." It is similar to AA's "spot check inventory" in moments of disturbance. Self-control begins by learning to take a pause between an arising urge and the automatic behavior. You then have an opportunity to wield your sword of critical discernment. Shantideva, the author, advises:

When the urge arises in the mind
to feelings of desire or wrathful hate,
do not act! Be silent, do not speak!
And like a log of wood be sure to stay.

When an urge arises, such as anger, fear, or any other emotional reaction, there are four moments to intervene and gain control of yourself:

1) The urge begins as an inner tug, an ill-at-ease feeling, a sense of something wrong. Before a thought is formed in the mind, the reaction begins with an initial perception. Some sight, sound, physical sensation, or memory causes discomfort. Awareness of this initial discomfort can prevent an emotional avalanche from gaining momentum.

2) Next, a stream of negative thoughts begins to flow. Be aware of the spontaneous thoughts that accompany the discomfort. You may be unaware of these emerging thoughts which express some negative interpretation of the perception. Simply observing these thoughts keeps them from gaining power over your mind.

3) The stream of thoughts then becomes a torrent, taking the shape of horror stories. If you ignore the subtle thoughts that accompany your emotional reaction, your emotions will intensify and be prolonged. It is still not too late to catch, with your mind's eye, these arising thoughts and stop the avalanche of emotion. You can observe the pattern of these gathering thoughts, the negatively biased storytelling, and refuse to buy into it.

4) Finally, there is a moment when the urge leads to action, either fight, flight, faint, or freeze. You can interrupt the automatic chain reaction that has formed into an addictive habit. You can stop to consider what you value, the consequences of your behavior, and how you want to act. Even in the face of an intense emotion that seems overwhelming, you are not as helpless as you think. You are always free to choose how to act.

With practice, you can train your mind to pay close attention to moments when your anger begins to rise. In the process, you will not only manage your anger's expression, but learn the message of the emotion.

In steps six and seven, you continue the work of house cleaning. You again become an observer of yourself. You look closely at what prevents you from surrendering your faults. Becoming ready, willing, and able, you make a committed decision to allow yourself to be transformed into the image of your true self.

Dennis Ortman, Ph.D.

10

Help Others:
Forgiving Yourself and Others

*Step Eight: "Made a list of all the persons we had harmed,
and became willing to make amends to them all."*

*Step Nine: "Made direct amends to such people whenever possible,
except when to do so would injure them or others."*

*"The quality of mercy is not strain'd,
It droppeth as the gentle rain from heaven
Upon the place beneath. It is twice blest:
It blesseth him that gives and him that takes."*

—William Shakespeare

Growing up in a home where temper outbursts were common, anger imprisoned me—and I didn't even know it. I also held the key to my freedom. However, it took me a long time to use it. After being ordained a priest, which was the fulfillment of a lifelong dream, I had a vague sense of unhappiness. Everything was going so well in my life that I couldn't imagine any reason for feeling depressed, so I began therapy. At times I felt like a volcano ready to explode. Yet, the meaning of those rumblings escaped me.

My therapist invited me to explore the anger that occasionally broke the surface. I talked about my father's drinking and his drunken rages. I acknowledged the terror I felt as a child and slowly uncovered the rage I had toward him. The sadness also emerged, how much I missed being close to him. I learned I suffered from a "father hunger" because of his emotional absence.

Over time, I sorted out my confused feelings and longings for intimacy. My father died of cancer when I was a teenager. I despaired of reconciling with him. My therapist suggested I try to learn as much about him as I could. I knew he was a veteran of World War II, a survivor of seven campaigns in his three years of service. I read numerous books about the war and what soldiers experienced. I came to realize that my father suffered from post-traumatic stress disorder and likely drank to drown the horrors of the war. Gradually, my anger turned to compassion. I discovered the key to my own freedom from the grudge I held against him—forgiveness. Now, I look for ways of saying, "I'm sorry."

After a thorough house cleaning, you are ready to make a fourth leap of faith, to help yourself by helping others. Taking your moral inventory, you realized the roots of your anger in self-centered fear and the harm it caused you. The eighth and ninth steps invite you to look backward at your relationships, how your anger has damaged them and how you can repair the damage. The

Steps/Traditions book states, "Every AA has found that he can make little headway in this new adventure of living until he first backtracks and really makes an accurate and unsparing survey of the human wreckage he has left in his wake" (p. 77). Your efforts to clean house, then, naturally overflow into helping others and rebuilding relationships on the basis of your chosen values.

Anger breaks your heart and relationships. Forgiveness mends them. Acknowledging the harm done to yourself and others, you ask for and give forgiveness.

Forgiveness Heals

What is the forgiveness that heals the wounds of anger? The word "forgiveness" gives the clue to its meaning. "Fore-give" means "to give ahead of time." It is an act of generosity in giving a gift to the person who offended you. The offender does not deserve the gift and has not earned it. You do not overlook the harm he has caused you or minimize the damage. Instead, you make a decision to give up your anger toward him and the desire for revenge. You then try to replace that resentment with compassion and love.

Forgiveness usually does not happen all-at-once. It unfolds gradually, as you realize and embrace the pain of the wrong done to you. You feel the hurt deeply and grieve the loss of what was taken from you. Your anger covers the pain. However, over time, you realize the impact of the anger on your own wellbeing and decide to give it up. You look beyond your anger to the suffering it causes. Furthermore, you look beyond the harmful behavior to see the offending person who also suffers. Then, you decide to forgive, telling yourself, "I forgive because that's who I am. I'm better than the revenge I seek." Gradually, you transform the energy of anger into compassion and love, which matches your true self.

Forgiving frees you to live the present moment fully, according to your true nature. It releases you from the bondage to past hurts, which are kept alive in your memory when obsessing about them. The past no longer holds you hostage. Old patterns of reacting, of wound collecting and grudge holding, are given up. You are no longer bound by your negative thinking, which only harms you. Through forgiving, you drop the weight of wrath and live lightly.

Nonetheless, you may resist the impulse to forgive, engaging in a fight within yourself. For example, you may say:

"If I forgive, I'm condoning and excusing what the person did." To the contrary, authentic forgiveness involves acknowledging the harm done, not overlooking it. Forgiveness admits that the action was wrong and should not be repeated.

"I can forgive, but I cannot forget what was done to me." Forgiveness does not produce amnesia. It is only surrendering the anger and desire for revenge. Some hurts are so deep that they can never be forgotten.

"That person does not deserve my forgiveness for what he did." That is true. You are not obliged to forgive. Your forgiveness is a gift. However, letting go of your anger benefits both you and the offender.

"The harm was so great I could never trust that person again." Forgiveness does not necessarily lead to reconciliation, resuming the relationship. Sometimes the offense is so grievous and the offender so unrepentant and untrustworthy that you can only protect yourself by keeping a safe distance.

Begin with Yourself

The eighth step instructs you to make a list of those you harmed. The first person on the list needs to be yourself. You begin mending your own broken heart by forgiving yourself. *Emotions Anonymous* states clearly that before you can make amends with others you must acknowledge your own woundedness and need for healing: "Many of us realize the person hurt the most has been ourself, and we have to include our own name on the list. We may have hurt ourselves by blaming ourselves for things that were beyond our control or by judging ourselves too harshly. We must accept and forgive ourselves if we are to accept and forgive others" (p. 66).

Through your personal inventory, you realize that you are your own worst enemy. You are the persecutor who victimizes yourself by your anger and character defects. You may indulge in exaggerated self-blame, always feeling guilty. Often, you hold yourself to impossibly high standards and criticize yourself mercilessly for not reaching them. For example, Jerome, a college student, came to see me because he had suicidal thoughts. He said, "I can't stand my life. I don't want to live anymore."

When I asked him the reason, he said, "I can't do anything right. I'm failing in school. I don't have any friends. I push myself to do well in classes, but freeze up on exams. When I get behind on a subject, I tell myself I'll never catch up and just give up. My friends don't invite me to do things with them. I know I'm depressed and no fun. Who would want to be around me?"

I asked him what he expected of himself. He responded, "I expect to be perfect. Even though I know it's not realistic, I feel driven to be perfect. I have to have all As. When I struggle in a difficult class, the fear takes over that I won't succeed. That's when I give up."

I pointed out his all-or-none thinking and said, "What is perfection? It's only an idea in the mind and doesn't really exist. Can you give yourself a break for not accomplishing the impossible?" We then began working together to dismantle his perfectionist belief system that spawned his self-loathing.

If you tend to suppress your anger, you likely attack yourself mercilessly. To forgive others, you must first forgive yourself. That involves giving up the anger for not living up to your great expectations. If you remain stuck in self-revenge, you will not take care of yourself. You will not believe you deserve happiness. Forgiveness also means loving yourself wisely, living a healthy lifestyle. Alcoholics Anonymous warns that if you do not take care of your basic needs you risk a relapse. Those needs are defined by the acronym "HALT," which means, do not let yourself be hungry, angry, lonely, or tired. Do you take care of your physical, emotional, mental, and spiritual needs? If you neglect any of them, you risk relapsing into your anger addiction.

Interconnected

We treat others the way we treat ourselves. Conversely, the way we react to others reflects how we treat ourselves. We are not as separate as we think. If we come to forgive ourselves, we open our hearts to forgive others, who are really another self. At a deep level, we are all part of a whole, and the whole is reflected in each of us. Difference does not mean separation. Uniqueness does not suggest disconnection.

A traditional Jewish tale speaks about our interconnectedness. An old rabbi asked his students, "How can you tell when the night has ended and the day has begun?" Traditionally, that is the time for certain holy prayers. One student responded, "It is when you can see an animal in the distance and tell whether it is a sheep or a dog." The rabbi shook his head. Another student proposed, "It is when you can clearly see the lines on your hand." Again, the rabbi said, "No." A third student said, "It is when you can look at a tree in the distance and tell if it is a fig or a pear tree." "No," the rabbi answered. "Then, what is it?" the confused pupils asked. "It is when you can look on the face of any man or woman and see that they are your brother or sister. Until then, it is still night."

We are all members of the same human family. We have a single origin and share a common destiny. We all long for happiness and seek relief from suffering. More intimately, as Saint Paul suggests, we are members of one body. When one member suffers, all suffer. We are not as separate as we think.

Despite the inscription on our money, "One from many," our culture espouses a rugged individualism, which promotes an "us-versus-them" mentality. It proclaims that we are separate individuals who compete to be the best. Working together may make us stronger, but true strength comes from personal determination and hard work. "Looking out for number one" leads to more grabbing than sharing. The sense of connectedness requires a leap of faith to see through our cultural conditioning. That faith, however, can be verified by careful observation of how everything changes and arises through interacting.

Nevertheless, our essential connectedness is stated clearly in the golden rule, to which all the religious traditions subscribe: "Treat others the way you would have them treat you" (Matthew 7:12). The love commandment echoes this truth: "You shall love your neighbor as yourself" (Matthew 22:39). That means loving your neighbor as another self. There is an inseparable link between how we treat others and how we relate to ourselves. In caring genuinely for others, we care for ourselves; in loving ourselves, we love others. The opposite also holds true regarding hatred and judgment: "If you want to avoid judgment, stop passing judgment...The measure with which you measure will be used to measure you" (Matthew 7:1-2). The hostility and judgment we impose on others boomerangs back to us.

An acceptance of our essential unity enables you to forgive others. Forgiveness arises from the mind of acceptance. It is contrary to the mind of rejection that underlies your angry reactions.

Forgiving Those Who Harmed You

Instead of indulging the rejecting mind in self-blame, you can become stuck in blaming others. You can become preoccupied with how others have harmed you. They become your enemy. Keeping a grudge list, you wallow in self-pity. Then, guilt hides in the recesses of your heart. Recognize that the blaming holds you prisoner. However, forgiveness frees you from the scourge of anger, hatred, and resentment. You forgive others for your own sake, to give you relief.

To set yourself free, take a walk through your past, beginning with childhood. Recall those who harmed you and caused you suffering. This may be a painful walk, but take it with the confidence you gained in trusting your Higher Power. Look honestly at your personal grudge list. One by one, hold in memory each of those persons who caused you pain. Hold them gently. Recall the painful incidents and how the person offended you. Allow yourself to feel the pain and your anger. Notice the stories you tell yourself about how you were wronged, and let them go. Just feel deeply the pain and tell yourself, "It's okay to feel the pain; it won't control me." Watch the hurt, sad, and angry emotions arise and fall away. Reflect also on the wisdom of Lama Surya Das, the Buddhist teacher, "Forgiveness means letting go of the hope for a better past."

In your mind, tell the person how their behavior affected you, how it influenced your life. Imagine what you would say. Then put yourself in the place of that person. Try to imagine what that person was feeling, thinking, and doing when they harmed you. What motivated their actions against you? Did they realize they were hurting you? Imagine that person listening attentively to you expressing the suffering they caused you. Imagine also what that person would say to you now, aware of your suffering. You may want to write a letter to that person to express more clearly your feelings. You do not have to mail that letter.

Be gentle with yourself, then, as you recall painful incidents in your life. You must be careful in remembering the past, especially if you were traumatized by physical or sexual abuse as a child. The recollections may be too painful, too overwhelming, and cause flashbacks. If you begin to feel overwhelmed, stop immediately, take a deep breath, and try to calm yourself. Address the painful memories only when you feel strong enough and ready. Take the time you need.

Some memories of pain may hide and come to light interacting with others. During marital therapy, a man who had a temper told me he became upset whenever his wife delayed having sex. I asked him, "What bothers you about that?"

He said, "I feel rejected. I think that she doesn't care about me."

His wife quickly interjected, "I keep telling you how much I love you. It's just that sometimes I'm too tired for sex."

When I asked him where he got the idea his wife does not care about him, even when she repeatedly assures him of her love, he said, "I felt unwanted by my parents. They paid so little attention to me that I felt neglected. I thought something was wrong with me." Without realizing it, he was reliving in his marriage what he experienced with his parents. He recognized that he needed to forgive not only his wife, but also his deceased parents.

Letting go of the anger and hurt will set you free. Your heart will lighten. It will liberate you to love yourself again, unburdened by a buried guilt. Martin Luther King, the freedom fighter, said, "Darkness cannot drive out darkness; only light can do that. Hate cannot drive out hate; only love can do that." It also enables you to make proper amends. *Emotions Anonymous* states, "If we do not forgive others as they are, we will not make amends with dignity, self-respect, and humility" (p. 67).

Forgiveness is exercising the highest form of love, loving the enemy who does not deserve it. In an unexpected way, forgiving your enemy can make him a friend. The one who makes your life difficult becomes the occasion for you to grow. He becomes your beneficiary, because through your interactions, you confront your own weaknesses and learn patience. It is only through adversity that you develop strength and character. There is an ancient legend that a renowned teacher, named Atisha, purposely kept an obnoxious servant. Everyone asked him, "Why do you keep that miserable man?" He responded, "I'm grateful to him. He gives me the opportunity to learn patience."

Asking Forgiveness of Others

Your moral inventory made you aware of how you have harmed others. You need to ask them for forgiveness. That can be a daunting task because you feel so powerless. You can only humbly ask for forgiveness, never demand it. You do not deserve it. The offended party is free to give or withhold it. You may feel especially vulnerable in making the request.

Seeking forgiveness assaults your pride. It takes considerable courage both to ask for and receive mercy. Recall the story of Peter and Judas in the Christian Scriptures. After Jesus was arrested, Peter denied him three times. Judas had already betrayed Jesus by selling him out for thirty pieces of silver. Both were filled with remorse after their betrayals, yet responded differently. Peter wept bitterly and later proclaimed his love for Jesus three times. In contrast, Judas threw the silver in the temple and hanged himself. He imagined his sin was greater than God's mercy, unlike Peter who humbly accepted forgiveness. Peter realized that his sin was merely a drop in the ocean of God's mercy.

How can you prepare yourself to ask for forgiveness? The Steps underline, first, the need to recognize the harm your anger has caused others. During your moral inventory, you investigated and confessed the roots of your anger and the underlying character defects. You realized that self-centered fear and excessive desires fueled your anger and took many forms. Now look at how your anger affected others. Review your life and think about those you harmed, intentionally or not, by your anger in thought, word, and deed. Who are they? Consider the following observations and questions:

- How did your secret critical judgments affect others?
- Did you offend others through your speech: lying, gossiping, complaining, sarcastic comments, and so forth?
- Did you intimidate others through your temper tantrums to get your way?
- Did you engage in physically violent or intimidating behavior?
- What effect did your sullenness, emotional withdrawal, or silent treatment have on others?
- What unrealistic standards did you impose on others?

- What impact did your blaming and flight from responsibility have on others?

Be aware that your angry attitude may seep out and infiltrate your life in many subtle ways. For example, Clark, a sensitive man who admitted to being chronically critical, told me: "I went to the store and was offended by the rudeness of the cashier. I admit that I'm sensitive to disrespectful people and I take it personally. I hate going to the store because everyone is so rude. I stopped going to church because the people were so rude and hypo-critical. I'm even self-conscious where I live. My neighbors watch me, and I think they're judging me."

One by one, hold in memory those you harmed. Recall the circumstances, the repeat-ing situations, in which you caused that person pain. Bring to mind what you were experi-encing during those incidents, your anxiety, sense of desperation, and your selfish pursuit of relief. Put yourself in the place of the person you hurt and feel their pain. What did they experience? Imagine what they were thinking and feeling at the time. How was your action harmful to them?

Be gentle with yourself during these recollections. Avoid blaming yourself or refusing any responsibility. Allow yourself to feel genuine remorse, which opens your heart in com-passion. Such compassion is the only way to escape the prison of hatred.

Secondly, seek forgiveness only when you are ready. It is an intimate act of exposing yourself that may arouse an overwhelming anxiety. Anticipate your fears in approaching each person on your list and how you can keep yourself calm enough to speak from your heart. Of course, you must be sincerely sorry for what you have done. Otherwise, your deceit will only cause more harm.

Next, asking for forgiveness should be done face-to-face, not over the phone, texting, or through email. If you cannot meet with that person because of practical difficulties, you may decide to write a letter. One of my patients told me how she reconnected with an estranged friend by mail and felt immense relief. If the person is deceased or unavailable, you may hold that person in your mind, make a sincere apology, and pray for him or her.

Fourthly, make your apology specific, not general. Do not say, "Forgive me for whatever I may have done to hurt you." Before the meeting, have a clear idea of specific incidents, behaviors, or neglect that harmed that person. Do not make excuses for yourself. Speak simply, directly, and honestly from your heart, as best you can.

Finally, allow the hurt party to respond, and then listen. Resist the urge to become de-fensive if that person becomes critical of you. Your inner critic may be easily activated by any angry response. Most likely, the offended person will be surprised and grateful for your apology and quickly accept it. That person may even try to take some of the blame and ask for your forgiveness. Be open to whatever happens. Do not become fixated on a particular outcome, as is your habit. Let it be an intimate moment.

Breaking Bad, Making Good

For true repentance, I learned as a Catholic that I had to make "a firm purpose of amendment." Confessing my sins and asking for forgiveness was not enough. I had to be sorry and demonstrate it by my efforts to change my behavior. Recovery does not end with asking for forgiveness. A continual effort to break your habit of angry reacting and replace it with value-directed living is required. Only love overcomes hate. Habit change occurs in three steps: recognizing and investigating the habit, doing something different, and persisting in the change.

1. Recognize and Investigate the Habit.

Your anger has become a bad habit, hard to break. Loosening the grip of the habit begins by recognizing your unwholesome tendencies in using the natural energy of anger. Become acquainted with your personal anger style. Do you tend to indulge or suppress your anger? Are you quick-tempered or slow boiling? Do you tend to hang on to it or let it go quickly? How frequently do you have temper outbursts? How intensely do you feel and express your anger? Do you express your anger mostly in thoughts, words, or deeds? What triggers your angry reactions? What persons and situations touch tender spots that you need to defend? What costs and benefits do you derive from your anger?

Next, lovingly investigate your anger. Look deeply into your anger to discover the perceptions, beliefs, and expectations you entertain about yourself and the world. Pay particular attention to the stories you tell yourself when angry. If you observe closely how your mind operates, you notice that it plays tricks on you. You fantasize about how your world should be. That image comes from memories of the past, experiences of pleasure and pain. You expect the world to satisfy your needs for security, power, and affection in particular ways. When the world does not measure up to your expectations, does not give you what you want, you become distressed. Feeling powerless, you react with anger. The anger gives you the illusion of power. An AA slogan states, "The road to disappointment and resentment is paved with expectation."

As you explore your anger with your wise, open mind, you begin to withdraw the interest, energy, and attention you give your storytelling. You realize that the thoughts that feed your anger are like clouds, lacking any real substance. It is only your attention and belief that give them weight. That awareness causes the anger to loosen its grip on your life.

2. Do Something Different.

After recognizing the hollowness of your angry thinking and automatic reacting, you can choose to act differently. You may be so accustomed to reacting emotionally to situations that you do not believe you can choose to act otherwise. I often remind my patients of the AA slogan of seven Ts: "Take the time to think the thing through." I invite them to cultivate their wise mind of acceptance. I tell them, "Just step back and observe what you are doing and thinking. Ask yourself: Does this really make sense? What do I really want to do?"

You may especially feel powerless over your anger when confronted with someone else's temper. You are accustomed to reacting and retaliating. I often tell my patients the following story to affirm their freedom (1):

"One day, the Buddha was walking across a plot of land when a man angrily started shaking his fist in the Buddha's face, saying he had no right to be walking there. The Buddha looked at him and said, 'Tell me, if you prepared a lovely gift for someone and you reached out to give it to someone, but they refused to accept it, to whom would the gift belong?' 'To me, of course,' the man replied. 'Just so,' the Buddha said. 'I'm not accepting the gift of your anger. Therefore, it remains with you.'"

My patients are often stunned by this story. They exclaim, "How is this possible? It's so difficult not to react."

I tell them, "Of course. What makes you think it should be easy? However, you can learn, with practice, to cultivate your wise mind and decide to respond, not react in your default mode." I explain, "Anger is like a hot coal. If you accept it and react with anger, both of you burn up. But if you do not accept it, only the other person suffers."

Beneath anger is hurt. Beneath hurt is your tender heart, your sense of vulnerability. What triggers your angry defensive reaction is a perceived attack on your sensitive spot. Pay attention to your triggers: when you do not get your way, when you feel disrespected, criticized, unfairly blamed, rejected, and so forth. You do not have to get caught up in the pain and act in anger. You are free to respond with kindness, which arises naturally from your true self.

3. Persist in the Change.

Finally, you need to persist in your changes. Transforming bad habits into good ones requires time and effort. Have confidence that positive change is possible. Research demonstrates that the brain is more plastic than we realized. It is capable of change. Throughout life, learning creates neural pathways that lead to repeated behavior. Repetitive thoughts, emotional reactions, and behaviors reinforce those pathways. Because of the brain's plasticity, new learning is possible. As you open yourself to new experiences and ways of thinking and behaving, the old neural pathways are diverted and new ones develop. These new pathways, in turn, are reinforced with repetition until they lead, once again, to a new automatic behavior. The challenge of recovery is to remain open to new experience and to growth.

My patients tell me they recognize that they are not themselves when caught up in anger. For example, one man, who suffered from temper tantrums, said, "When I have my meltdowns, it's not me. I'm not in my right mind. It's as though I'm possessed, like the Hulk."

I encouraged him, "Then, just be yourself. Act in a way that is natural and meaningful to you. That behavior comes from who you really are."

There is a story from the Native American tradition about the inner battle with habits and the need for persistence:

"A tribal elder told his grandchildren: 'There's a terrible fight going on inside me between two wolves. One wolf represents pride, anger, greed, gluttony, envy, deceit, lust, sloth, and despair. The other stands for humility, patience, generosity, gratitude, serenity, courage, truthfulness, innocence, zeal, and hope. This same fight is going on inside of you and every living person.' The children were amazed by what their grandfather said and sat silently thinking about it. Then one child asked, 'Which wolf will win?' The wise elder responded, 'The one you feed.'"

If you continue observing yourself closely, you are aware of the fighting wolves within you. You also know which one aligns with your true self. You can choose which wolf to feed by cultivating your mind of acceptance. Be confident you can release anger's energy for constructive purposes. Through the struggle with unwanted habits, you acquire virtues that could not be achieved otherwise. Remember that no habit is stronger than you.

Paradox of Perfection and Imperfection

Your anger reveals your compulsion to live in a perfect world under your complete control. When others, or you, do not measure up to your high standards, your anger erupts. You can direct it against others or yourself. Our society also promotes constant progress in striving toward perfection. It proclaims, "Become better every day." Hearing that message only makes you feel worse. An impossible dream of how life should be possesses you. Compared to your ordinary life, you reject yourself and the world as hopelessly flawed.

Flaws, however, can hide beauty. There is a story about a famous artist. The city council of Florence purchased a six ton block of marble to create a monument for the city. They tried to commission the best sculptors in the city for the project. All refused, saying, "The marble is too imperfect. It will not be able to stand on its own." That huge block of marble sat in a field for 25 years. Then one day a young artist approached the council and said, "I'll make it into a masterpiece." When the huge block was delivered to his studio, the young man slept with it. Each night he hugged it and spoke to it, "What is crying out to be released from you?" After several weeks, he began his work. Two years later, he revealed his creation, which amazed the whole city. The statue was of David. The sculptor was Michelangelo.

Recovery presents you with a paradox in facing your flaws: "You are already perfect in your imperfection." As much as you hate your anger and your faults, your imperfections possess an unseen beauty. Look beneath the surface of your life. Look beyond and through your flaws. You were created perfect, with more goodness than you realize. You only have to act out of your true nature. Love yourself as you are, not the way you wish you would be. Through understanding and accepting your weaknesses, you gain humility. Simply being yourself can release a magnificent beauty and power the world needs to see. Your unique beauty will be expressed through your imperfect, unique human personality.

Practice: Love Enemies Meditation

Another practice to help you on the path toward self-acceptance is meditating on select passages from the Bible. I suggest that you meditate on the following verses from the Gospel of Matthew (5:40-48). Jesus is addressing the crowd and you personally. Consider the words a personal message from Jesus to you:

> "You have heard that it was said, 'You shall love your neighbor and hate your enemy.' But I say to you, love your enemies and pray for those who persecute you, that you may be children of your heavenly Father, for he makes his sun shine on the bad and the good, and causes rain to fall on the just and the unjust. For if you love those who love you, what recompense will you have? Do not the tax collectors do the same? And if you greet your brothers only, what is unusual about that? Do not the pagans do the same? So be perfect, just as your heavenly Father is perfect."

The following steps summarize a meditation practice called "lectio divina"(2), which is a prayerful reading of the Scriptures:

1) Sit comfortably in a quiet place with your Bible. Take a few moments to quiet yourself and focus on being present in the moment. Be aware of God's presence and love for you. Ask Him to open your mind and heart to His words.

2) Read the words of the passage slowly. Allow the words to penetrate your soul. Consider them Jesus addressing you in your here-and-now situation, with all your concerns. If a phrase jumps out at you, allow yourself to linger over it. Savor the phrase, taste its truth. Repeat it to yourself, allowing its truth to reach a deeper level within you.

3) Next, respond spontaneously to the words. Let the feelings of gratitude, consolation, and even discouragement emerge without hindering them. Reflect for a moment on your reactions to the words and what it reveals about you. Let your concerns show themselves.

4) After a time of reflection on the word and your reactions, rest in silence. Let all the chattering thoughts pass and do not dwell on them. Be still and sense God's loving presence. Enjoy the stillness and peace, which may be unfamiliar to you. The silence may be uncomfortable for you at the beginning. Stay with it. Extend the quiet time, from just a few minutes to as long as you like, as you become more familiar with this practice.

5) Finally, end the session with a spontaneous prayer of thanksgiving. Carry a meaningful phrase with you throughout the day.

The Twelve Steps flow in an alternating rhythm of contemplation and action. Reflecting on how you have harmed yourself and others by your anger, you take action. You decide to forgive yourself and others and experience the power of forgiveness to bring forth new life. In loving the enemy within and outside yourself, you are healed, made whole. In caring for others, you care for yourself. Love transforms the world.

Dennis Ortman, Ph.D.

Power of Self-Examination:
Making Friends with Yourself

*Step Ten: "Continued to take personal inventory and
when we were wrong, promptly admitted it."*

*"The impediment to action advances action.
What stands in the way becomes the way."*

—Marcus Aurelius

When I was ordained a priest, I had deep longings to belong to a family. Alcoholism ravaged my family. All of us children moved away for geographical safety. I entered the high school seminary at the tender age of 13, with youthful zeal to serve God as a priest. I found in the Church a family, a secure place to belong. I fell in love with my parishioners and served them with dedication. However, the succession of painful moves from one parish to another took its toll. It caused me to relive the trauma of my own broken family. I felt desperately lonely.

I felt redeemed when some parishioners made their home my home. Surrounded by love, over time, I fell in love. With my growing dissatisfaction with the celibate lifestyle and my desire for my own family, I made a painful decision at age 40 to leave the active ministry. I got married, went to school, and became a psychologist.

Despite the strain of adjusting to a new life, I felt content. I enjoyed the family closeness I so desperately desired. However, a black cloud rose in my paradise. My 16 year old stepdaughter resented me as an intruder. On good days, she referred to me as "the bald bat." On bad days, she radiated hostility and called me unmentionable names. I was frustrated and discouraged. My illusion of family bliss was being put to the test. It was an opportunity to grow in patience and kindness or withdraw into self-pity.

Marathon Running

You may have hoped that recovery would be a quick sprint to the finish line of relief from your anger sickness. Unfortunately, it turned out to be a marathon, requiring more time, effort, and endurance than you expected. You may have had delightful moments in the zone, but often it was hard work. That should not be a surprise. You likely struggled with your anger for many years and tried various strategies to manage it. Perhaps you hoped that working the steps would provide a quick and easy solution to your suffering. You hoped for a lasting cure, but none came.

When you started working the program, you may have had some personal goals that were not clearly articulated. Three typical approaches come to mind: settlers, fire extinguishers, and constant watchers. Two are dangerous, and one is the narrow way that leads to new life. Settlers tell themselves, "I've worked on myself enough to gain some control over my anger. I'm satisfied with where I'm at. I don't need to work on it anymore." Their goal is symptom relief. They only want to manage their anger enough to keep them out of trouble. They may believe that when their temper subsides they are cured.

Fire extinguishers say, "I'll get help when I get in trouble again with my anger." They work the program only as needed, when a crisis arrives, because it demands so much effort. They may recognize their anger as a relapsing illness and address the problem only during relapses. Often, they need the encouragement of others to get help.

Constant watchers admit, "I know I have a problem with deep roots. I have to constantly be on guard and watch myself closely. I know there is no cure for my anger addiction. I must keep working on myself." They recognize that working on the character defects that underlie their angry reactions is a lifelong process. They realize that life always requires them to learn, change, and grow. To ignore this demand puts them at risk of relapse.

You are now entering a new phase of your recovery, the ongoing, life-long management phase. How will you respond? Fortified by the wisdom and power gained in working the steps so far, you can become a constant watcher and deepen your healing and growth. Your recovery from addiction to anger will always be a work in progress. "We shall look for progress, not for perfection," the Steps/Traditions book admonishes (p. 91).

Triad of Recovery

To continue and deepen recovery, the Twelve Step program suggests a balanced attention to three practice areas: "Trust God; clean house; help others." As mentioned previously, the first three steps involve coming to trust in God, your Higher Power. In steps four through seven, you work to clean house, to acknowledge the character defects expressed in your anger. You help others and yourself in making amends and coming to forgiveness.

This triad of practices is not something new. They are rooted in ancient religious traditions, passed on from generation to generation. All the major religions, Hinduism, Buddhism, Judaism, Christianity, and Islam, teach its followers to pray, fast, and give alms. Prayer is not simply a mouthing of words. It is a trustful opening of the mind and heart to God and dedication to following His will. Fasting is not only abstaining from food. It symbolizes a willing self-renunciation of any distorted desires that interfere with doing God's will. Almsgiving to the poor represents the generous willingness to serve others, and not only oneself. These traditional practices lead to exploring three crucial questions:

- Humble fasting asks, "What illusions are keeping me stuck?"

- Heartfelt prayer inquires, "Who am I?"

- Generous almsgiving questions, "What am I meant to do with my life?"

The last three steps summarize the previous nine, apply them to daily living, and spotlight these crucial questions. Your anger unbalances your life. It gives you an emotional hangover. The continuous practice of the steps promises to restore harmony, peace, and balance. Step ten begins by recommending a regular personal inventory and prompt admission of faults. The Steps/Traditions book underlines its importance: "Then comes the acid test: can we stay sober (calm), keep in emotional balance, and live to good purpose under all circumstances?" (p. 88). Why is that ongoing inventory so important?

Necessary Trials

You need the inventory because your life inevitably falls out of balance. After all, you are only human. Your anger is a gift because it alerts you to the imbalance. However, you often feel like you are living on a battlefield and do not like it. Competing desires are at war within you, trying to gain your attention. You interact with others, who mirror your inner competition to get your needs met. Often, you compete for the same prize and fight. That battlefield can be a tightrope on which you are straining to keep your balance.

By some unforeseen happenstance, you attract situations that expose your inner conflicts, causing pain. As much as you hate it, the pain is a gift. It wakes you up. Constant pleasure and success would only keep you asleep. Those difficult, painful situations challenge you to grow, recover your balance, and find wholeness.

Relationships are an example of a challenging, yet rewarding, circumstance. Working with couples for many years, it strikes me how often opposites attract each other. If you married someone just like you, your clone, boredom would soon set in. Unconsciously, you seek someone different, which brings some excitement into the relationship. You seek a partner who complements you, makes up for your hidden weaknesses. Initially, the relationship may be exciting. Infatuation carries you along, but over time, your partner's differences may drive you crazy. The relationship may become a battlefield, rather than a place of refuge. A power struggle to change the other may begin, or you can wake up to what needs to change in yourself.

For example, Kevin and Cathy came to therapy on the brink of divorce. Cathy complained, "I'm sick and tired of doing everything around the house. Kevin leaves messes everywhere. I'm constantly picking up after him and reminding him of what needs to be done. I'm exhausted and resentful."

Kevin chimed in, "Cathy doesn't know how to relax and have fun. She's always working and telling me and the kids what to do. I wish she would just chill out."

I asked when the problems began. Cathy said, "In the beginning, I loved that Kevin was so carefree. We went out all the time and had fun."

Kevin nodded his head and added, "I loved that Cathy was so responsible and hard-working. I knew she was someone I could count on."

"When did your appreciation for each other change," I asked.

"When we had children," Cathy responded, "but Kevin kept wanting to have a good time."

"Cathy became intolerably anxious and serious. She forgot how to laugh," Kevin complained.

What you initially loved about your partner often becomes what you have difficulty accepting later. A loving relationship exposes the strengths and shadow sides of you and your partner, the aspects of your personality that are hidden. In the above example, clearly Cathy needed to learn how to relax, while Kevin was challenged to be more responsible.

Bob and Rosemary are another example. Bob explained, "What I loved about Rose was how close she was to her family and friends. I envied that. I was never close to my family and had few friends. Instead, I loved to work and devoted myself to my career. Rose knew that my career and providing a good life for the family was important to me. When I received this great job offer, something I always dreamed of, Rose flew into a rage. We would have to move, and she was adamantly against it."

Rosemary told her side, "I loved that Bob was so hardworking, stable, and responsible. We were always poor growing up, and I looked to marry a stable guy. But Bob has become so money driven that I can't stand it. All he thinks about is work. Now he wants to move for the sake of his career and uproot us from our family and friends."

Both Bob and Rosemary are being challenged to grow in unexpected ways. Bob is invited to connect more emotionally with himself and others. Rosemary needs to become more independent and care for herself.

These unavoidable trials present you with a choice. They test your freedom. You can resist looking at yourself and try to change others, the past, or unwanted circumstances, or you can view them as wonderful opportunities to look within and rebalance your life. You can take the inventory of others and remain stuck, or you can work on your own inventory and become free.

From a larger perspective, "karma" states that every action has consequences. The universe is moving toward harmony, unity, and balance. Any action that upsets the movement toward wholeness evokes an opposite correcting reaction. You can understand your trials as necessary for your growth toward wholeness if you pay attention to the message. For couples, that means focus on changing yourself, and not your partner, to find happiness. Mooji, the wise mystic, advised, "Don't waste time watching and reacting to the mind of 'others.' Your own mind causes more trouble than the minds of everyone put together" (366).

The founders of the great religions experienced necessary trials before beginning their missions. The Spirit drove Jesus into the desert to be tempted by the devil. He was offered possessions, power, and prestige, but chose to worship God only. Mara, the deceiver, approached the Siddhartha Gautama, later known as the Buddha, while in meditation. He showered him with sensual delights and raging wars, but Siddhartha remained serene. Moses wandered in the desert with his people for 40 years. He was tested with hunger and idolatry before entering the Promised Land. Muhammad confronted his own self-doubts and lack of faith when he met the Archangel Gabriel who brought God's revelation. Meeting the enemy face-to-face prepared them to know who they were and what their mission in life would be. They embraced their demons and learned from them.

Learning from the spiritual greats, how are you to face your necessary trials?

Keep Alert and Aware

Face your trials by keeping your eye on the ball. That way you stay in the game. In baseball, the players must be alert when the ball is in play, or disastrous things can happen. They may strike out at the plate or get hit in the head. They may make an error in the field, misplaying or dropping the ball. To play the game of life well, you have to keep aware of yourself and your reactions to your surroundings.

Step ten invites you to stay alert and aware by making the inventory of the fourth step a regular practice. It continues the work of housecleaning in the present moment. *Emotions Anonymous* states: "In doing the fourth-step inventory we dealt honestly with our past so that we could free ourselves from it. This tenth-step inventory helps us deal with the present as we cope with daily living. Now that we are aware of our human imperfections, we realize we can easily fall back into our old ways of thinking and behaving" (p. 71-72).

What is required to stay alert and aware? You simply have to be quiet and open to the present moment. For us Americans, accustomed to staying active and busy, that can be challenging. Patients often ask me to give them some exercises to work on between sessions. I tell them, "Just pay attention to yourself." They are often surprised because they see themselves involved in some self-improvement project in therapy. They want work assignments with measurable results.

"How do you do that?" They ask.

I tell them, "Simply be quiet and notice what is going on in your mind. In the next session, we'll talk about what you are observing. Just get to know yourself."

Being open to whatever arises in the mind without judging it is difficult for many. Your mind is like an empty pot. It can be so full of your own preconceived ideas, opinions, and judgments that there is no room for anything new. It can be filled with cynical, poisonous ideas that interfere with openness. The pot can also have holes in it so nothing is retained. You are so busy and distracted that nothing sticks in your mind. Only a mind that is empty and quiet can learn.

It is also difficult for many to stay focused on the present moment. Your mind jumps around like a wild monkey swinging from branch to branch in the jungle. It moves to past memories and then leaps to future expectations, bouncing around between the two. One patient began each session with a ritual, which reflected how stuck he was in the past. He asked, "What's new?"

I responded, "This moment is new. It has never existed before in the history of the universe and never will again." Only the present moment is real. The past is gone, and the future does not yet exist.

To what specifically do you pay attention?

Examine Your Reaction Chain

Pay attention to what arises in your mind in the moment. The tenth step suggests making a regular "spot check inventory" when you sense anger arising. Your addiction to anger does not possess you all at once. Each hostile episode has an accumulating effect. Each angry episode begins like a snowball that starts small and gathers momentum to become an avalanche that buries you. If you pay close attention to tiny twinges of agitation, you will notice the rising dark clouds that eventually become a terrible storm.

You can work with your anger by observing closely the signs and symptoms of the rising storm. If you can interrupt the chain reaction of growing distress, you can protect yourself from being lost in the storm. That chain is breakable. A saying from an unknown source (1) describes the links in the reaction chain within your mind and their connections. I have added two links:

Watch your physical sensations; they become emotions.
Watch your emotions; they become thoughts.
Watch your thoughts; they become words.
Watch your words; they become actions.
Watch your actions; they become habits.
Watch your habits; they become character.
Watch your character; it becomes your destiny.

When your mood is changing, take a zoom lens look at your experience. Notice the unique way that you experience anger, so you can recognize the emerging pattern of reacting more quickly the next time it occurs:

BODY SENSATIONS: Your body holds the pain of the losses you experience and never forgets. Your muscles constrict, preparing for fighting, flying, or freezing. Where do you feel tension most? Do you feel knots in your stomach, pressure in your head, or pain in your back or neck?

EMOTIONS: The four main emotional groups are sad, mad, glad, and scared. What combination do you feel mostly? Notice their fluctuations, their ebb and flow, and variations in intensity. You may detect subtle feelings within feelings, such as shame, guilt, envy, pride, resentment, greed, lust, and so forth. You may miss feelings of delight, elation, gaiety, enjoyment, pleasure, and so forth. What is your predominant feeling? Hurt underlies your anger. The hurt reveals your tender heart and your vulnerability.

THOUGHTS: Based on past experience, you spontaneously interpret events as favorable, unfavorable, or neutral. These interpretations interact with your spontaneous emotional reactions. When you are angry, the thoughts run in a negative direction with unrealistic expectations and harsh judgments. You see the offender as an enemy who purposely harmed you. You also feel entitled to seek revenge to right the imbalance. What automatic negative thoughts arise in your current situation? Notice the judgments. What expectations do you entertain for yourself and others? How realistic are they? What happy memories and blessings of loved ones do you overlook?

WORDS: Your thoughts take shape in words both inside and outside yourself. What internal dialogue is going on in your head? How do you speak to other people? Do your words build up or tear down? What beliefs about yourself, relationships, and the world do you express?

ACTIONS: Actions arise from impulses deep within you. They are also shaped by your feelings, motives, and thoughts. How do you treat yourself and others? If you are caught up in anger, you tend to neglect your basic needs. As AA observes with the acronym HALT: "Don't be hungry, angry, lonely, or tired." Do you care for yourself properly?

HABITS: Repeated actions become habits. What habitual patterns of feeling, thinking, and behaving do you observe? If you are angry, you may either suppress the uncomfortable feeling or indulge it in temper outbursts or grudges. Do you engage in any addictive behaviors to self-medicate your pain?

CHARACTER: You naturally reflect on your life experience and tell yourself stories about yourself. The narratives make sense of the chaos of your experience and give you an identity. What stories do you tell yourself about who you are? Those who are angry tend to see themselves as fearful victims, proud bullies, or guilty caretakers. How do you see yourself?

DESTINY: Your choices have consequences, some foreseen and others not, creating your character and destiny. The values you choose give direction to your life and shape your destiny. What do you value? What are your priorities in life? What is the gap between the way you would like your life to be and the way it is? You can change your destiny by aligning your life more with your values than the dictates of your angry reactions.

As you become proficient, with practice, in making spot checks, you will become familiar with your tendencies. You can interrupt the automatic reacting, stop, think, and choose to act in a way that makes sense to you. Awareness gives you the power to break the chain of reacting. It frees you to live according to your values, which arise from your true self. In the process of observing your reactions, the gap between the urge and the action broadens. You can more promptly recognize, understand, and admit your fault. Then you can make amends without carrying the unnecessary burden of guilt.

Alfred, traumatized and hot-headed:

"I was molested as a child. The pain never leaves me. I was shocked one day to see my molester's name on Facebook. I had a flashback and became enraged. Because I had been working on myself, I knew what was going on, so I took some time to calm down and think things through. My first impulse was to destroy him by telling his wife. I stopped to consider my motive and what I hoped to accomplish. In telling his wife, would I be vindictive or protective, so other kids will not be in danger? Should I alert her? What would be the best way? I'm still figuring out myself and what to do. I'm confident I'll find an answer."

Sharon, fearful and submissive:

"I'm divorced, and my teenage daughter is refusing to be with me on weekends. She has become just like her father, who is a bully. I'm terrified that I will never see her again. If I demand she come home, she may hate me forever. If I do nothing and give in to her stubbornness, as is my habit, she will just stay with her father. I went to see

an attorney to clarify my rights. I'm determined I will not give in to my fear and I will find an effective way to assert myself. I can be patient as I work through this."

What's the Harm?

The awareness you bring to your spot check inventory possesses the natural energy of anger. It is a blazing fire. Used wisely, it can give light to see yourself more clearly. The energy of the emotion warms your heart to be compassionate with yourself and others. It can also burn away the false illusions that keep you stuck. One illusion that enslaves the anger-prone is the sensitivity to being harmed and wronged.

When my patients come to me complaining about being hurt by someone, I invite them to tell their story of being wronged. I then ask them, "What was the harm?"

The question startles them, and they may respond, "My feelings were hurt."

I assure them they are entitled to all their feelings and that there is no wrong feeling. I then add, "You feel what you feel and need to be honest about that. The next step is to understand precisely why you feel that way. Ask yourself what that feeling is saying about you." Our emotional reactions come from early emotional programming and result from ways we interpret events. I explain to them, "It is not the event, what happened to you, that caused the harm, but how you reacted to it. If you believe it was the event, you make yourself a victim of circumstances. You are at the mercy of what happens to you."

For example, Natalie told me, "I became enraged with my friend when she commented about my weight. I felt insulted."

"What was the hurt?" I asked.

"She hurt my feelings. I was teased as a child for being overweight, and my parents constantly made comments about it. I'm sensitive about how I look."

"Who do you think is really judging you about your weight," I enquired.

"I guess I am," she responded.

I explained, "The criticism of others affects us to the extent that it echoes what we are already telling ourselves. What would happen if you accepted the fact that you weigh what you weigh?"

"I suppose I would not care what other people thought or said. I know I'm self-conscious about what people think of me. I take things personally," she acknowledged.

Upon closer examination, the problem for Natalie was not her weight or her friend's comment, but her expectations and harsh self-judgment. That leads us to the truth that we cause our own problems by how we think about ourselves and the world. Marcus Aurelius observed this almost two thousand years ago, well before the invention of cognitive therapy. He said, "Disturbance comes only from within—from our own perceptions...Choose not to be harmed—and you won't feel harmed. Don't feel harmed—and you won't be" (4:3i and 4:7). Shantideva, the eighth century Buddhist teacher, affirmed this insight. He wrote:

We are like senseless children
Shrink from suffering, but love its causes.

We hurt ourselves; our pain is self-inflicted!
Why should others be the object of our anger? (4:45).

The realization that you are the cause of your own suffering, and not someone else, is liberating. You cannot change other people or many of the circumstances of your life. However, you can change yourself, particularly your attitude towards what happens to you. If you believe you can only be happy if others or circumstances change, you make yourself a victim of outer uncontrollable events. Your wellbeing depends on what is outside of you rather than within.

Marcus Aurelius offered another startling and liberating piece of wisdom. He wrote in his *Meditations* (4:8 and 9:4), "It can ruin your life only if it ruins your character. Otherwise it cannot harm you—inside or out...To do harm is to do yourself harm. To do an injustice is to do yourself an injustice—it degrades you." What others or the world does to you does not affect the core of who you are. It cannot touch your character. How others act reflects their character. If they intend you harm, it degrades them. You are only responsible for your own behavior and building your own character. Your intentions and actions affect you deeply. If you act according to your chosen values, you thrive. If you react in ways that you disapprove of, you violate yourself.

The practice of making a regular personal inventory reminds you to know yourself and to take full responsibility for your own life. Socrates observed, "The unexamined life is not worth living." Knowing yourself and being responsible, you are free to be your natural self. You suffer if you resist the natural flow of your life, not accepting yourself as you really are. Making friends with yourself, with all your imperfections, brings contentment.

What I Learned

Relationships never solve problems. In fact, relationships do not even cause problems for us. We do that to ourselves. One of the supreme benefits of taking the risk of intimacy, though, is that it exposes our hidden tendencies to the light of day. It shows us who we really are—if we pay attention. Then we can work on our automatic reacting with our conscious mind and allow our true self to emerge.

When I married and had a family, I thought I had arrived, redeemed from the loneliness of a celibate life. I expected contentment and peace. My stepdaughter's hostility toward me shattered that illusion. My frustration and whining revealed that I was stuck. I imagined that belonging to a loving family would make me happy. Without realizing it, I discovered that I was looking for something outside of myself to bring happiness. I was looking for some external validation of my worth. "If others love and accept me, then I must be okay," I secretly thought.

My stepdaughter gave me a great gift in her rejection. Her behavior invited me to confront my own reactions and be honest with myself. I was looking for happiness in the wrong place. Instead, I had to find it within myself, by making friends with myself. I had maintained the illusion that I needed to belong to a family. The truth was that I needed to learn to be comfortable in my own skin. I had to take ownership of my own life, not depending on others to satisfy my needs.

I am immensely grateful to my stepdaughter, who has grown to love me, as I love her. Her gift of anger helped to set me free. It challenged me to drop the illusions that kept me from simply being myself.

Paradox of Loss and Gain

The threat of losing something important to us gives rise to anger. We may fear losing self-esteem, power, control, or anything we deem essential to our wellbeing. The anger empowers us to fight for ourselves. Our culture reinforces aggressive action. We are promised, "You can have it all and have it now; be the best and don't settle for less; know no limits." We are told to keep adding more for happiness: possessions, power, and achievements. Such high expectations inevitably lead to disappointment and resentment. We are then encouraged to work harder, fight more, and never give up.

The paradox of recovery suggests another program for success: "We lose to gain." Recovery from any addiction, including anger, requires less, not more, a giving up rather than chasing after. Anger reveals what we desire desperately, imagine we need to be happy, and fear losing. Anger gives us the illusion of power when we feel powerless. To find contentment, then, we must subtract, rather than add. Taking our moral inventory when anger arises, we learn what attachments keep us stuck. It might be an excessive desire for security, power, or affection. To gain freedom, we need to drop the judgments, unwholesome habits, and ideas of perfection.

Mooji, the spiritual teacher, said, "You never lose what you give; you only lose what you try to keep" (547). The secret to happiness is in letting go of our excessive desires for personal pleasure and expanding our desire to care for others. When we give generously to others, we are enriched. When we cling to ourselves, we feel deprived and resentful.

Practice: An Evening Inventory

The Steps/Traditions book recommends, in addition to the spot-check inventory, a regular evening inventory-taking. It suggests drawing up "a balance sheet for the day," not only what is done in red ink, but also in black ink. Your anger and fear draw you to the negative. An accurate balance sheet of your life must include the positive, what you have done right, for a more balanced perspective.

A Japanese practice called "Naikan," which means "looking inside," can be helpful for this balanced accounting at the end of the day (2). The practice invites you to reflect on the past twenty-four hours of your day and ask yourself three questions: 1) What have I received? 2) What have I given? 3) What difficulties have I caused?

What have I received?

Unfulfilled expectations fuel your anger. You focus on what is missing, not on what is present. Your glass is always half empty, never half full. You see the void, not the abundance. Because you pay so much attention to what you do not have or fear losing, you ignore what you already have. Your life is full, and you do not even recognize it. At the end of the day, pause to reflect on all the good things you received. Contemplate the simple pleasures: kindnesses from those you encountered, a joyful moment with the family, a call from a friend.

Noticing your blessings can inspire an attitude of gratitude to offset your preoccupation with things going wrong.

What have I given?

When angry, you become more demanding that others give you what you want. You may expect others to adjust their lives to your sensitivities. Self-preoccupation and a sense of entitlement may creep into your life. To confront this tendency, it is important to consider what you did for others. Note even the simple things: a friendly greeting at the store, listening to a friend's troubles, doing your work with a joyful heart.

Noticing your own spontaneous generosity can increase your self-confidence that you have much to offer.

What difficulties have I caused?

Your harsh self-judgment can make you either blame others or yourself for your misery. True humility invites you to see yourself accurately and recognize the impact of your behavior on others. At the end of the day, honestly admit to yourself how you may have harmed others by what you have done or not done for them. Perhaps you nursed old wounds or entertained harsh judgments of others. Allow feelings of remorse to rise in your heart. That will motivate you to find a way to repair the damage, both to yourself and the other person.

The ongoing effort to transform your unhealthy habits to beneficial ones releases a new energy. You recognize how chasing your illusions, the butterflies of happiness, has drained you. When you drop those illusions, you feel free and alive. Your heart is open to embrace the world. Seeds of joy begin to blossom.

Dennis Ortman, Ph.D.

Power of Prayer:
Making Peace with God

Step Eleven: "Sought through prayer and meditation to improve our constant contact with God as we understood Him, praying only for knowledge of His will for us and the power to carry it out."

"We are both human and divine. Human troubles compelled the wise to discover their divine nature."

—Mooji

I imagined myself an expert on prayer. Raised a Catholic and ordained a priest, I learned a lot about how to pray. As a young child, each night I knelt beside my bed with my parents, recited the "Angel of God" and asked God's blessings on our family. Of course, we prayed grace before all our meals. When I entered Catholic grade school, we were taught "Our Father," "Hail Mary," and the rosary. We were introduced to all the sacraments and rituals of the Church.

Entering the seminary, I graduated to other more sophisticated prayer forms. Each morning we spent an hour in meditation in the chapel, struggling just to stay awake. We learned to appreciate the richness and wisdom expressed in the Sacred Scriptures. We were taught ways of praying with the Scriptures to uncover deeper meanings and listen to God speaking personally to us through the texts. Instead of just saying prayers, we also prayed spontaneously from the heart. We also learned the value of listening over speaking in prayer, and spent more time in silent reflection.

As a priest, I joined a fraternity with other priests. We met monthly for silent reflection before the Blessed Sacrament and shared a review of our lives. Daily, I spent an hour in prayer. Once a month, I made a retreat, a day in the desert, where I was alone and quiet with myself for a day in prayer. Reflecting on the Scriptures for preaching enriched my personal spiritual life. I learned the value of silence, listening, and being alert to God's presence in ordinary daily events. I aimed for a prayerful attitude, a conscious contact with God, in all my activities.

After becoming a psychologist, I looked into world religions. A summer spent in India many years ago planted seeds of interest in Eastern philosophy. In my explorations, I discovered a wisdom that showed a path to healing, growth, and freedom. I followed my breath and became mindful. I learned many meditation techniques to cultivate concentration and insight. I also found practices to develop self-awareness, empathy, and compassion.

Now, I see myself as a novice in prayer. I fumble and fail to keep conscious contact with God. My heart is not always in it. I become distracted and lose interest at times. Most embarrassingly, my way of life does not match my prayerful aspirations. However, I find consolation that God does not give up on me, even when I ignore him. A Hindu proverb wisely stated, "When we take one step toward God, He takes seven steps toward us." Even if we cannot find the words or heart to pray, the Spirit aids us. St. Paul wrote, "The Spirit too helps us in our weakness, for we do not know how to pray as we ought; but the Spirit himself makes intercession for us with groaning that cannot be expressed in speech" (Romans 8:26). So I try never to give up.

Step eleven expresses the second major theme of the Steps: "trust God." It invites you to continue deepening your relationship with your Higher Power, with God, that you began in the second and third steps. A thread of prayer also runs through all the steps, the spirit of the Serenity Prayer.

The Steps/Traditions book underlines the benefits and necessity of prayer for your continued growth: "We want the good that is in us all, even in the worst of us, to flower and grow. Most certainly we shall need bracing air and an abundance of food. But first of all we shall want sunlight; nothing much can grow in the dark. Meditation is our step out into the sun"(p. 98). In the sunlight, you discover the deeper meaning of three questions:

- Who am I?

- Who is God?

- What is His will for me?

Prayer Problems

When I struggled with praying in the seminary, my spiritual director always assured me, "Pray as you can." There are as many ways of praying as there are individuals attempting it. Nothing is more personal than prayer. It only takes desire, time, and effort.

The sticking point for many in prayer is their view of God. Some see God as more welcoming than others. As mentioned previously, God can seem judging, forgiving, critical, or distant for different people. Some imagine God in personal terms, while others think of the Divine as an impersonal Force in the universe.

The God you pray to may reside in heaven. You pray, "Our Father who art in heaven." This God, who is above and beyond you, may seem unreachable in prayer. He is infinitely above you. You do not know how to communicate with Him. Your religion may ask for a humble submission, which may be offensive to you, particularly if you are preoccupied with a sense of personal powerlessness. Or you may see God as a harsh and critical Judge. He is like a celestial Santa Claus who monitors your behavior, warning, "You better watch out, you better not cry..." Again, you do not spontaneously approach such a God or openly trust Him. Research shows that a majority view their personal God in such negative terms.

Eileen, a guilt-ridden Catholic:

"When I was growing up, the priests and nuns were put on a pedestal. We thought of them as close to God, His representatives on earth, so we listened closely to what they said. Their word was God's word. I attended Catholic schools. I had many painful experiences of the priests and nuns being harsh and strict. The nuns hit us with rulers for the smallest offenses. The priests warned us about the dangers of sex, mortal sin, and the fires of hell. Fear and guilt controlled us, and we became compliant children. Now, it's hard for me to pray to a loving and forgiving God, the way He's preached about today. Catholic guilt runs deep."

Because of disaffection with such a negative view of a personal God, you may look for the Divine around you and throughout nature. Your God is Divine Energy, Creative Intelligence, Universal Mind, or the Spirit of Nature. God seems closer, permeating the universe. However, this impersonal God may not be any more approachable than a remote, judging Supreme Being. How can you communicate with Something? How can you be sure that the "Divine It" cares about you as a person? Is the universe you trust in hostile or friendly? You can find plenty of evidence for both positions. Your faith provides no secure answer.

There is a third way to view God, which may be more hospitable to prayer and the desire "to improve our conscious contact with God, as we understood Him." The third place to look for God is within yourself, hiding in the depths of your consciousness. In your personal search for Truth within your own experience, you may find a God with whom you can connect. How do you make conscious contact with this God within?

Prayer: Be Here Now

"Be here now," Ram Das, the spiritual guru of the 1960s taught. Just "be." That sounds simple, but is very difficult. We are accustomed to staying busy and productive. When you ask someone how they are, they automatically respond, "Keeping busy." Our culture teaches us to define ourselves by "doing," rather than "being." Our value comes from our achievements. To be inactive is to be lazy. However, reaching the Divine Presence within requires that you go against the grain and stop. Be quiet and still. Silence is golden. Stop talking and running around, and just listen. You do not have to do anything.

"Be here." We are always moving, wanting to be someplace other than where we are—physically, economically, emotionally, and every other way. We are not content where we are. Consequently, we seek geographical cures for all our ailments. We imagine that elsewhere is a more congenial, happy place. Marcus Aurelius observed this obsession with moving two thousand years ago: "People try to get away from it all—to the country, to the beach, to the mountains. You always wish you could too. Which is idiotic: you can get away from it all anytime you like. By going within. Nowhere you can go is more peaceful—more free of interruptions—than your own soul" (4:3). Simply be present in your body.

"Be here now." Our minds are like wild monkeys in the jungle, jumping from branch to branch, from the past to the future and back. What we avoid is the present moment. Why? Because we do not believe the present moment is enough, so we dwell in the past or imagine a better future. We remember and plan. In thinking about the past, we focus on what we missed, what could have been, "If only..." Jumping to the future, we worry about what can go wrong, asking ourselves, "What if...?" Regrets and hopes occupy our mental space. However, only the present moment exists. The past is gone, and the future does not yet exist. Prayer invites you to enter deeply into your reality, which is the present moment, and give up your time travel. An AA slogan states, "Yesterday is history, tomorrow is a mystery, today is a gift—that's why it's called the present."

Thich Nhat Hanh, the renowned Buddhist monk, founded a movement called "Engaged Buddhism." He grew up in Vietnam and protested the war, calling both sides to reconciliation. He was nominated for the Nobel Peace Prize for his efforts. Hanh believed that true meditation/prayer enabled the person to become more fully engaged in life, which included the political and social arena. He affirmed that our true home is in the here and now. This is the place of our happiness and peace. He taught a simple practice centered on the breath:

> "Breathing in, I calm my body.
> Breathing out, I smile.
> Dwelling in the present moment
> I know this is a wonderful moment."

Meditation: Who Am I?

Another avenue "to improve our conscious contact with God" within is through meditating on the question, "Who am I?" There is no more intimate question. You find the answer by paying close attention to your own experience. Just observe yourself.

In making your moral and personal inventories, you observe yourself closely. With practice, you learn to step back and become a detached observer. What do you see during an angry episode? You sense a rising storm that begins with an initial discomfort signaling that something is wrong. You notice how your body reacts, becoming tense and restless. You feel the agitation arising and permeating your whole body, preparing you to fight. Perhaps you notice underlying feelings of hurt, shame, or fear. Angry thoughts fill your mind, crowding out peaceful ones. You think about how you were wronged and want vengeance, some way to restore the balance of power. You remember all the past hurts that the current one triggers. As the rage gathers momentum, you observe the stories you tell yourself about how you are an innocent victim of a guilty villain. You rationalize that you have a right to retaliate and may begin plotting your revenge.

I invite my patients to enquire into who it is that experiences their anger. That may seem like a strange question. You immediately respond, "Of course, I'm angry?" But who is the "I" that is angry? For example, Mark, an admittedly sensitive man, complained during a session that he felt insulted that a friend did not invite him to a party. He was angry about it. As we explored his angry reaction and hurt feelings, he said, "People tell me I'm too sensitive. I become offended even when they do not intend to hurt me. I take it personally. I can't help myself. I just react with hurt feelings and anger."

Anger Anonymous

"Who is experiencing the anger? Is it really you choosing to be angry?" I asked.

He thought for a moment and said, "I guess it's not really me. It's as if I'm possessed by some hidden force that makes me react with anger." I suggest that it is the force of habit that comes from early emotional programming.

With another patient, Bethany, we explored who it was that was harmed by her husband's temper outburst. She said, "My husband has such a terrible temper when he doesn't get his way. I've been working hard not to react with anger and fight back. It never helps. It only causes the argument to escalate."

"Can he really harm you by his anger?" I asked.

"I'm not afraid he will physically harm me, but I am frightened," she responded.

"But can his anger really touch the core of who you are as a person? Can it affect your character?" I enquired.

"When you stop and think about it, he can't really affect my character by his behavior. Only I can do that when I react in ways that I don't feel good about," she said thoughtfully.

As you observe all your angry reactions, you realize something important. "That is not me. I'm not that person consumed by anger," you tell yourself. "I'm better than that." You realize that the sensations, feelings, and thoughts are not the real you. They may come from you as you react to unpleasant events, but they do not define who you are as a person. Since you can stand back and observe the distress in your body and mind, you are separate from the distress. You are something more, beyond all the mental drama.

As you observe the passing thoughts and feelings, you recognize that they are like clouds that come from you, but are not you. As the observer, you are the spacious blue sky. Obviously, you cannot stand back and observe the self who is observing. You cannot be an object to yourself. An eyeball cannot see itself. However, you can have an intuitive sense, a feeling of being an "I" that is aware. Who are you, then? You are that pure awareness, that unlimited capacity to observe and investigate what you perceive. That awareness is a blazing fire that exposes and burns away illusions. The thoughts and feelings you notice are like waves in the ocean that rise and fall, but you are that vast ocean.

Sensing yourself as the spacious sky and vast ocean, you realize that your true self is timeless and boundless. Your awareness reaches eternity in its openness to truth, goodness, and beauty. When you view awareness from a religious perspective, you recognize its Divine qualities. Many religions proclaim that we are "made in the image and likeness of God." Your ability to know, love, create, and choose makes you God-like. Thomas Merton, the well-known monk of Gethsemane Abbey, eloquently stated: "Therefore there is only one problem on which all my existence, my peace and my happiness depend: to discover myself in discovering God. If I find Him I will find myself and if I find my true self I will find Him" (1).

The founders of the great religions spent time in prayer and meditation. Through that experience they discovered their true identity. They are role models for their followers. Jesus spent time in the desert and was baptized by his cousin John. He heard a voice from heaven, "You are my beloved Son. My favor rests on you." Siddhartha Gautama meditated under the bodhi tree, was tempted by Mara, and arose as the Buddha, "the awakened one." While praying in the desert, Moses encountered a burning bush. He experienced God's presence, who revealed His name, "I Am Who I Am." Moses became, at that moment, "the giver of God's Law." While praying in a cave, the Angel Gabriel appeared to Muhammad, gave him God's revelation, and made him "the prophet." In a similar way, through prayer and meditation you experience who you really are and who God is.

Through prayer and meditation you gain:

- Inner peace and joy—that you are made for happiness, not misery.

- Freedom from all bondage to thoughts, habits, automatic reactions.

- Awareness of shared Divine life—a true self that is timeless, unchanging.

- Connection with all—that you are not a separate self.

- Knowledge that you are loved, loving, and lovable by nature.

Prayer Changes Us, Not God

The eleventh step instructs, "praying only for knowledge of His will for us and the power to carry it out." There is no greater gift. When you pray from the heart, you realize your true self. Instead of playing God, chasing after power and glory, you recognize you are God-like. You can let go of your self-centered strivings and simply be yourself. I often remind my patients, "Therapy is not creating a better version of yourself. It is removing any obstacles that prevent you from simply being yourself." God's will is that you be yourself. Be the way you are. You do not have to be different. Release the power within yourself. St. Irenaeus, an ancient Church teacher, said, "The glory of God is man (the person) fully alive."

If you are simply, effortlessly being yourself, how will it look? How do you show your God-like qualities?

1. Enlarging Your Consciousness

In your anger, you can observe two minds in conflict. On the one hand, there is the ordinary mind that rejects what does not match its expectations of how the world should be. It judges quickly. It is preoccupied with being hurt and sees others as the enemy. Thoughts of retaliation fuel the anger. The focus narrows to the past harm and restoring lost power. On the other hand, you observe from a mind of acceptance that embraces all of your experience. It withholds judgment and excludes nothing. Loving thoughts create a sense of joy. A battle is going on between these two minds. If you simply recognize the emptiness of your mind of rejection, see it as "stinking thinking," you can let your higher consciousness shine its natural light. That is true enlightenment.

Your natural mind of acceptance, your true consciousness, has several qualities that make you fully alive:

- Embraces life as it unfolds without expectations.

- Observes without judging.

- Sees the big picture, that everything belongs.

- Engages the present moment fully with creativity.

- Has a friendly attitude toward all.

- Seeks to create unity.

- Loves first and last.

2. Living with Unconditional Friendliness

When you cultivate a mind of acceptance, your relationships change. The attitude of loving acceptance begins with yourself and radiates out to others. Your heart opens to intimacy. Natural bonds develop based on openness rather than fear. During an interview, the Dalai Lama was asked, "Do you ever get lonely?" He responded simply, "No." The commentator was surprised because the Dalai Lama lived in exile from his homeland, separated from his closest family and friends. He was also unmarried. The interviewer asked the reason for his surprising lack of loneliness, especially since we live in a society in which isolation and loneliness are pandemic.

After a moment of thought, the Dalai Lama responded, "I think one factor is that I look at any human being from a more positive angle. I try to look for their positive aspects. This attitude immediately creates a feeling of affinity, a kind of connectedness. And it may partly be because on my part, there is less apprehension, less fear, that if I act in a certain way, maybe the person will lose respect or think that I am strange. So because that kind of fear and apprehension is normally absent, there is a kind of openness" (2).

The mind of rejection focuses on the negative and is quick to feel offended. It sees the other as a competitor for limited resources. An us-versus-them mentality predominates. Because you judge others harshly, you expect others to do the same. Fear of being exploited or rejected grows. You feel isolated. In contrast, the mind of acceptance promotes compassion for yourself and others. You see the other as a beneficiary who is open to a friendly relationship like yourself.

There is a Buddhist parable that shows the power of acceptance that begins with seeing yourself as you are. One day, as the Buddha was sitting under a tree, a young, trim soldier walked by. He looked at the Buddha, noted his full girth, and said, "You look like a pig!" The Buddha looked up calmly and responded, "You look like God!" Startled by the comment, the soldier asked, "Why do you say that I look like God?" The Buddha replied, "We don't really see what's outside ourselves. We see what's inside us and project it out. I sit under this tree all day and contemplate God. So when I look out, that's what I see. And you must be thinking about other things."

We see others as we see ourselves. When you are a hostage of hostility and suspicion, what do you see? You see the other person as a threat and keep yourself on guard. A fog of fear hangs between you. If you view yourself a victim, you see others as persecutors and resent them. Your anger will then make you their persecutors. If you view yourself as powerless and needing to prove your strength, you encourage others to test you. You invite others to treat you the way you treat yourself.

In contrast, if you acknowledge your God-given greatness, you act with a magnanimous heart. The *Tao Te Ching*, the book of ancient Chinese wisdom, expresses the transforming power of self-awareness, "When you realize where you come from, you naturally become tolerant, disinterested, amused, kindhearted as a grandmother, dignified as a king" (22).

3. A Forgiving Heart

If you live with unconditional friendliness toward yourself and others, forgiveness comes naturally. After all, you were made in the "image and likeness of God," who is merciful and forgiving. You recognize that your anger at being harmed hurts you. As Marcus Aurelius observed, "How much more damage anger and grief do than the things that cause them" (11:18). Because you value your own wellbeing, you give up the anger for your own sake. You replace the anger with compassion, which then increases your own joy.

If you hang on to the anger, you are stuck. One woman held a grudge against her husband because he was a workaholic and didn't help raise the children. She felt overburdened and resentful caring for their three children alone. She nurtured the resentment. Over the years, it turned into a hidden guilt. She did not recognize the guilt, however, but felt extremely anxious. She exclaimed, "I always imagine the worst happening, as if some terrible punishment awaits me." I pointed out the hidden guilt for her anger and said, "The key to your own happiness and peace of mind is forgiving your husband."

When you live from your mind of acceptance with unconditional friendliness, you have the capacity to see beyond. You can look beyond your own faults and not become discouraged. You see your essential goodness, that you are better than your behavior. You can look beyond the harm the other person inflicted on you. That person shares in your own glorious and frail humanity. Mother Teresa, in speaking about her work among the poor, used to hold up her hand and raise one finger at a time as she said, "You do this to me." She was referring to the words of Christ in Matthew's account of the last judgment. "Whatever you do to the least of my brothers you do to me." Mother Teresa saw herself and others as "another Christ" worthy of love.

4. See a Wonderful World

Often on my drive to work I hum Louis Armstrong's inspiring song, "What a Wonderful World." It captures the joy I feel when I am in touch with my true self. When I maintain a prayerful attitude, I sense the timeless, boundless "I" that underlies the passing chaos of my life and thoughts. I feel a sense of connection with my deepest self, with others, and with the whole world. In fact, the universe reflects the goodness and beauty I see in myself. I can see beyond the ugliness portrayed in the news and see the heart of the world. It shares in Divine Life.

Mooji, the Jamaican poet-mystic, expresses the personally experienced beauty of life:

The value of life will be determined
by the value you place upon yourself, which, in turn,
depends on what or who you believe you are.
When you discover yourself
to be beyond name, form and conditioning,
life sparkles from the inside like a celestial diamond (595).

Seeing the beauty in life frees you to become engaged with the world and love it. Authentic prayer draws you into the world, not away from it. You are not afraid, so you do not have to dominate or control the world. You can let it unfold naturally and try to live in harmony with it. You have an intuitive sense of how to use the energy of your anger. You know when to speak up or stand down. Life flows freely through you, with no unnecessary resistance.

Paradox of Forgiving and Being Forgiven

When you pray the Lord's Prayer, you willingly put yourself in grave peril. You ask God to forgive you to the extent that you forgive others, praying, "Forgive us our trespasses as we forgive those who trespass against us." If you do not forgive others, you ask God to hold your sins against you. That puts pressure on you. Your eternal salvation is at stake.

The eleventh step presents another paradox of recovery: "We forgive others to be forgiven." Observing your experience closely, you notice the devastating effects of hanging on to your anger. It makes you sick in body, mind, and spirit. Medical research documents a long list of illnesses related to suppressed anger: heart disease, ulcers, cancer, back pain, and so forth. The black dog of depression and guilt may plague you. Negative and paranoid thoughts ward off a sense of contentment and peace. Your spirit is robbed of love and joy. Others shun or fight you, and you suffer the hell of isolation. You do not need God to punish you for your grudges. You do it to yourself.

Fortunately, there is a way out. The remedy for the poison of anger is forgiveness. It replaces the malice with benevolence. Because love and compassion reflect your true nature, you feel joy. You no longer feel the physical tension of preparing for fight or flight. You can relax in your body, feeling a sense of wellbeing. Thoughts of peace and love fill your mind. You experience a freedom from slavery to your emotions and can reach out to others. Your kindness, in turn, attracts kindness from others. Intimate connections can flourish. Without the water of mercy and compassion, no relationship can survive and grow. The grace and blessing of forgiveness is a taste of heaven here and now.

Practice: Centering Prayer

Father Thomas Keating, a Cistercian monk, developed a method of prayer to foster a contemplative attitude in your daily life. It is an attitude of being fully present in each moment of your life and aware of God's loving presence. It also keeps you close to your true self. When your life feels out of balance, it can stabilize you. His prayer method is called "Centering Prayer," and it opens your mind and heart to deepen your relationship with God and yourself (3). These are the guidelines for the prayer:

1) Choose a sacred word as a sign of your intention to surrender yourself to God's presence and action in your life. Spend some time in prayer and reflection to find a word that inspires you. It might be a word from Scripture, such as Father, Lord, Jesus, or Mother Mary. It might be a word that expresses your highest aspirations, such as Love, Trust, Faith, Courage, Hope, Peace, or Let Go. Choose a word that has personal meaning for you, expressing your desire for communion with God.

2) Go to a quiet place where you will be alone. Sit comfortably with your eyes closed. Close your eyes to focus your attention on the stillness within you without outer distractions. Be relaxed, sitting with your back erect. Breathe deeply. Then introduce your sacred word and repeat it to yourself slowly. Let the repetition help you focus on your center, where you sense God's loving presence.

3) Allow yourself to enter more deeply into the silence within you. Thoughts, feelings, sensations, and desires will inevitably arise. Do not fight them. Simply let them pass and keep your attention focused on the sacred word. During the prayer, even the sacred word may disappear. Gently let that pass also.

4) At the end of the prayer time, spend a few moments in silence. Sense that you are resting in God, and God is dwelling within you. You are one with God. That is your true nature. Then, slowly open your eyes and resume your activities with an uplifted mind and heart and a sense of gratitude.

Spend at least 20 minutes in centering prayer. You can extend the time as you become more comfortable with the stillness and silence. Throughout the day, during your normal activities, take a moment to center yourself and be fully present, as you were during the prayer time.

I add one word of caution. If you have been traumatized, an extended period of silence may be overwhelming for you because of the painful memories that may emerge from deep within your unconscious. Stop the practice if you are feeling overwhelmed. Return if and when you are ready.

With step eleven, you cultivate your relationship with God, your Higher Power, Ultimate Reality, through prayer and meditation. Finding yourself, you come to know God. In believing in God, you discover your deepest self. That accurate self-awareness finds expression in your pursuit of your unique mission in life.

Power of Giving:
Connecting with Others

Step Twelve: "Having had a spiritual awakening as a result of these Steps
we tried to carry this message to others suffering anger,
and to practice these principles in all our affairs."

"Vision without action is a daydream.
Action without vision is a nightmare."

—Japanese proverb

I believed God called me to be a priest. I admired the priests in our parish and got to know them personally. In the third grade, I became an altar boy. I felt close to God around the altar, reciting the Latin prayers I studied so diligently. When I was ordained a priest several years later and worked in parishes, I felt like I found a home. I loved the ministry. I knew I was born for this. I was doing what I was meant to do with my life, living out my God-given vocation.

When I left the active ministry to be married at age 40, I felt lost. Being married and having a family brought me joy. However, I felt a void and missed the priesthood. I needed a work of service to be fulfilled. What did God want me to do? Having a job to make money did not interest me. Pursuing a career in which I could advance and gain prestige was not my goal. I wanted work that would be a vocation, a life task that both matched who I was as a person and was a way to make a difference in the world.

I knew I wanted to work in a helping profession that challenged my intellectual abilities. Having grown up in an alcoholic family, I wanted to help those who suffered what I had suffered, so I entered a clinical psychology program and specialized in treating the dually diagnosed, those suffering from both substance abuse and emotional problems.

Now, after being a psychologist in private practice for nearly 25 years, I believe I found a vocation similar to what the priesthood was for me. I am helping others, and myself, in a meaningful way. I bring a spiritual dimension to my work. It is only that the form of my service has changed. I begin each day with a prayer of dedication, reminding me of the gifts I have received and desire to share with each of my patients. My prayer is: "As the earth gives us food and air and all the things we need, may I give my heart to caring for all others until all attain awakening. For the good of all sentient beings, may loving kindness be born in me."

Step twelve expresses the third major theme of the steps: "Help others." It encourages you to put into daily practice what you began in steps eight and nine, making amends and building relationships. Reaching out to others, the step promises, is the only path to a joyful life. The Steps/Traditions book states: "The joy of living is the theme of AA's twelfth step, and action is the key word. Here we turn outward toward our fellow alcoholics (sufferers) who are still in distress. Here we experience the kind of giving that asks no rewards"(p. 106).

If you are anger addicted, however, you experience little joy in living or active giving. The Steps give you hope of freedom to be yourself.

Stuck

Suppressed rage keeps you stuck. It can show itself in many forms, especially in a self-punishing anxiety. The judge comes and condemns you without mercy. Turning the anger inward, self-loathing consumes you. The resulting guilt and anxiety paralyze you. You cannot make a decision. Nothing brings you joy. You do not know who you are or what makes you feel alive. Disconnected from yourself, you have no idea what you are meant to do in your life.

For example, Marjorie came to me because she suffered crippling anxiety. We had been meeting for over a year when she complained, "My anxiety is worse than ever. I can't sleep. My stomach hurts all the time." When I asked her what was going on, what she was afraid of, she responded, "I can't make a decision. I'm miserable in my marriage. We're always fighting, just like my parents used to fight. I can't give up seeing Paul. I don't know what to do." Marjorie had been involved in a secret affair with Paul for many years.

I repeated to her what we had discussed many times, "You know you will have some peace when you make a decision, whether to end the marriage or the affair, or just be on your own."

"I just can't decide because I don't know what I want. In fact, I don't know who I am anymore," she complained.

"You know one thing about yourself, though. Living a double life is not who you are," I said.

When you live in contradiction to yourself, you pay a severe price. You betray yourself. You direct rage against yourself in guilty feelings and lose a sense of who you are. The pain, however, can be a call to growth.

I recently attended a workshop by Fr. Richard Rohr, a Franciscan priest and author of many spiritual books. He related that he was on the Oprah Show one time and told her, "When you are over 30 years old, you cannot learn anything from your successes, only from your failures." Oprah was shocked and asked him to explain. Rohr said, "When you are young, you need successes to build your self-confidence. But when you are older, you learn from failure, pain, and defeat. Success and pleasure keep you stagnant, just moving along. But failure and pain teach. They cause you to look inward, explore, and search for relief."

Marjorie's pain was an invitation to growth. I told her, "You will make a decision when you are miserable enough."

"How miserable do I have to be?" she asked.

"Only you can know that," I responded. Marjorie was ripe to be set free. It was only a matter of time—and willingness on her part. As AA observed so astutely, you have to "hit bottom" before you can begin recovery. Anger, whether indulged or suppressed, will invariably invite you to wake up.

Spiritual Awakening: Three Questions

Recovery begins with an awakening of the spirit of your true self. What does it mean to have a spiritual awakening?

The Steps/Traditions book offers a helpful definition: "When a man or woman has a spiritual awakening, the most important meaning of it is that he has now become able to do, feel, and believe that which he could not do before on his unaided strength and resources alone. He has been granted a gift which amounts to a new state of consciousness and being"(p. 106-107). *Emotions Anonymous* adds: "Whatever form it may take, our awakening contains a characteristic attitude change. We have become less obsessed with our problems and pain and more open to other people" (p. 79).

The spiritual awakening is here described as "a new state of consciousness" and "an attitude change." Albert Einstein famously remarked, "The significant problems we face cannot be solved on the same level of thinking we were at when we created them." That new kind of consciousness is an awareness of life from a larger perspective, accepting rather than rejecting life as it is. It involves a paradigm shift from a closed-minded judgment and rejection to an open-minded embracing of reality, which leads to gratitude and generosity. Some may object, "There's a fine line between being open-minded and having a hole in your head." Nevertheless, seeing deeply that everything belongs sets you free. Even the pain, failure, and defeat you experience can be stepping stones to new life.

Step twelve suggests that a spiritual awakening occurs as a result of working the steps. There is a logic and flow to the steps. From facing where you are stuck, you discover your true self, and then act accordingly. Working the steps, you address three questions that wake you up.

The first question: "Where am I stuck in my life?" Steps 4-7 and 10 raise this soul-searching question. Through your personal/moral inventory, you regularly ask yourself what inhibits your growth. Some self-obsession keeps you from growing up. Your anger, as much as you hate it, reveals what you desire desperately and fear losing. You are always angry about something. Almost always, you are angry because you are not getting what you want or you are receiving what you do not like. Everyone who struggles with excessive anger is like a two year old involved in a power struggle with life.

When you bring the burning light of awareness to the excessive desires and fears that underlie your anger, you begin to set yourself free. You may discover strong needs for security, power, or affection. Your "stinking thinking" is then exposed. You imagine that you will be happy if these desires are met. Observing and investigating yourself closely, you see the falseness of your beliefs. I tell my patients, "Being aware of your angry reactions is not like turning off a light switch. It is dialing down a dimmer switch." You can turn down the mental/emotional energy you invest in your negative thinking. Slowly, you see the emptiness of your distorted desires, see them as illusions that captivate you, and lose interest. You can then tell yourself, "It's really no big deal that I don't get what I want."

The second question: "Who am I?" Steps 1-3 and 11 address this important question. Through prayer and meditation, you discover who you really are beneath all the garbage of your distorted desires. You imagine yourself seeking a treasure that is always there for the taking. By stilling all your raucous thoughts, you sense the presence of what is timeless, boundless, and changeless. It is your pure awareness that cannot be defined or limited. It is your consciousness that reaches toward and participates in the Divine. Mooji, the Zen master, ironically expressed this truth: "It is not the person, but the consciousness that wakes up from this mess, and when it wakes up, it realizes this so-called mess is divine" (664). Saint Paul, reflecting on his life, observed, "I have been crucified with Christ, and the life I live now is not my own; Christ is living in me" (Galatians 2:20).

The third question: "What am I meant to do with my life?" Steps 8-9 and 12 suggest this question. When you understand your character defects and who you really are, your unique mission in life becomes clear. It naturally unfolds. You simply become transparent in your actions, being who you are. Often you complicate the process with rules, laws, and commandments of right behavior. However, if you are in touch with yourself, whose true nature is love, you just spontaneously respond to the needs of the situation. St. Augustine, the reformed sinner, taught, "Love and do what you will." Again, Mooji poetically teaches: "True love, peace, joy, wisdom and lasting contentment do not require any effort in themselves. Why? Because they are the natural fragrances inside your very nature, and what is natural is also effortless and need only be discovered" (636).

The founders of the great religions modeled this path to a spiritual awakening. Tested, they became aware of their identity, and their mission unfolded. Jesus was tempted by the devil in the desert. When baptized, he experienced himself as "God's Beloved." Then he began his ministry, preaching, "Reform your lives and believe the good news." Siddhartha Gautama meditated under the bodhi tree to discover the secret to the relief of suffering. After facing Mara, he rose as "the Awakened One," the Buddha. He then gathered his former friends at Deer Park to teach the four noble truths for the relief of suffering. Before leading his people through the parched desert into the promised land, Moses encountered God in a burning bush. He was chosen to set his people free and be "the Law Giver." He proceeded to present the Ten Commandments he received from God to the Jewish people. Muhammad struggled with the idolaters of Mecca. Praying in a cave, the Archangel Gabriel called him to be "the Prophet" and gave him the mission to recite God's Revelation as recorded in the Koran.

Family First

Bill Wilson, the cofounder of AA, followed in the footsteps of these spiritual leaders. Alcohol tested him; he acknowledged himself an alcoholic and became a missionary for recovery. After Bill Wilson "got religion," he became sober and began to turn his life around. He looked for a way to have "a quality sobriety," without the emotional hangovers of resentment, pettiness, and fear. He met with other struggling alcoholics and formulated the Twelve Steps for recovery. He believed that alcoholics could understand each other in ways that no one else could. They shared an experience with alcohol that bonded them. He created a fellowship, a place for alcoholics to meet and support each other. A key to recovery, he discovered, was overcoming the self-centeredness that spawned the addiction.

Helping others was the way out, so in the twelfth step, he underlined the need "to carry this message to alcoholics." You also have a gift in your anger sobriety. The message you carry is the power of forgiveness. You can help others who suffer from an addiction to anger.

I suggest you begin at home. Anger tends to be a family affair. There may be a genetic predisposition towards a quick temper, and certainly parents role model under or over-controlled anger to their children. The anger sickness passes on from one generation to the next. In your recovery, you can help break the family pattern. You carry the message, not by your words, but by your actions.

For example, Gina came to see me to help manage her own and her family's anger. She said, "I was raised in a hot-headed Italian family. It's no surprise I married a man with a temper. We've had our arguments. I've learned to take time outs and to calm myself with him. What is intolerable now is how he yells at the kids. I can see how afraid they are of him, and I want to protect them. It reminds me, of course, of when I was a child and my parents yelled at me. I just scream at him when he yells at the kids."

"Does it help when you get out of control like him? How are you different from him?" I asked.

"I guess I'm no different," she admitted.

"What are you role-modeling for the kids?" I added.

"I just feel so powerless and don't know what to do," she confessed.

"Perhaps we can figure out a way for you to remain calm and set limits," I suggested. We then worked on strategies for her to remain calm and discuss rationally with her husband more effective ways of disciplining the kids. She knew from years of experience that yelling and arguing did not work. She acknowledged her need to forgive her husband for his temper.

Passive-aggressive displays of anger can be just as devastating within families.

Stephanie, an anxious, over-controlled mother:

"I was a shy child. My father was an ambitious, hard-working man. He pushed me to excel at everything I did, at school and in sports. He kept telling me it was for my own good, so I could be the best person I could be. The problem was, I later discovered in therapy, that what he wanted me to do did not match who I was as a person.

I was a quiet, sensitive person who enjoyed the arts. He wanted me to be a successful business woman so I wouldn't have to depend on anyone and could support myself. Ironically, I grew up lacking self-confidence. Now, as a parent, I'm sensitive to how each of my children are different. I respect their temperaments and encourage them to pursue their own interests."

Make a Peaceful World

Step twelve finally invites you, "to practice these principles in all our affairs." Like a stone thrown into a pond, the impact of your renewed life has a ripple effect. Making peace with yourself extends from person to person to change the world. Mother Teresa was often criticized for not becoming politically involved to change social structures. She insisted she was not a politician or social worker. Her calling was to love one person at a time. The power of her selfless love, embracing the poorest of the poor, has, indeed, changed the world.

Working the steps, you begin by facing your own shadow and coming to forgive yourself. Making amends, you forgive those who harmed you and ask the forgiveness of those you offended. The prayer of St. Francis becomes your aspiration:

"Lord, make me a channel of your peace—
that where there is hatred, I may bring love—
that where there is wrong, I may bring the spirit of forgiveness—
that where there is discord, I may bring harmony—
that where there is error, I may bring truth—
that where there is doubt, I may bring faith—
that where there is despair, I may bring hope—
that where there are shadows, I may bring light—
that where there is sadness, I may bring joy.

Lord, grant that I may seek rather to comfort, than be comforted—
to understand, than be understood—
to love, than to be loved.
For it is in self-forgetting that one finds.
It is by forgiving that one is forgiven.
It is by dying that one awakens to Eternal Life."

Being true to yourself, you may discover a calling to become involved in the wider community. Become involved only if it comes naturally to you when you have awakened spiritually. You cannot force social activism, telling yourself, "I should do this." If you do, you will do violence to yourself. Acting out of your true self happens effortlessly. Of course, you expend effort, but it does not drain your spirit. Like the Boy's Town image of a boy carrying another boy, who comments, "He ain't heavy. He's my brother." When you act out of your true nature, it only brings joy. It may be a tired joy, but it is a deep contentment, nonetheless.

Models of Forgiveness

I enjoy reading the biographies and autobiographies of individuals who have changed our world. I am eager to learn their secrets. The following are some I admire most.

1. The Dalai Lama, a man of compassion.

Tenzin Gyatso was born into a poor farming family in Tibet. At a young age, he was designated by the spiritual leaders of the community as the 14th Dalai Lama, which means "Ocean of Wisdom." The Dalai Lama is recognized within the Tibetan Buddhist community as the reincarnation of the Bodhisattva of Compassion. The young Tenzin was trained in the best schools and became the spiritual leader of Tibet.

His remarkable personal qualities were put to the test when China invaded Tibet in 1949, and the people lost their freedom. When the Tibetan people rose up in rebellion ten years later, they were brutally crushed by the Chinese. The Dalai Lama, 24 years old at the time, fled across the rugged Himalaya Mountains to seek refuge in India. He witnessed the violence against his people and the dismantling of their sacred places. Separated from his family, he was forced to live in exile.

The Dalai Lama had every reason to be outraged at the Chinese. However, he has repeatedly said he forgives them with no reservations. He stated that his greatest fear is that he lose compassion for them. He recognizes that in their hatred they are suffering. The Dalai Lama explains the reason for his forgiveness: "If I develop bad feelings toward those who make me suffer, this will only destroy my own peace of mind. But if I forgive, my mind becomes calm. Now, concerning our struggle for freedom, if we do it without anger, without hatred, but with true forgiveness, we can carry that struggle even more effectively. Struggle with calm mind, with compassion" (1).

2. Nelson Mandela, a freedom fighter.

Nelson Mandela was born with the proud rebelliousness and stubborn sense of fairness of his father, a tribal chief in a small South African village. Instinctively, he knew in his heart that he was born free. He had the desire to extend that freedom to the whole nation that was under the apartheid rule. He wrote, "I knew as well as I knew anything that the oppressor must be liberated just as surely as the oppressed. A man who takes away another man's freedom is a prisoner of hatred...The oppressed and the oppressor alike are robbed of their humanity" (2).

Mandela fought to free his people from their racism and eventually became the first black president of South Africa. His strategy was a tactical use of nonviolence and noncooperation in the tradition of Gandhi, his predecessor in the struggle for freedom. He broke selected laws in urban areas and encouraged strikes throughout the country. He was arrested for conspiracy to overthrow the state and served 27 years in prison.

Mandela refused to be a prisoner of hate and had compassion on both his prison guards and white persecutors of his people. He believed in the essential goodness of humanity. He wrote: "I always knew that deep down in every human heart, there is mercy and generosity. No one is born hating another person because of the color of his skin, or his background, or his religion. People must learn to hate, and if they can learn to hate, they can be taught to love, for love comes more naturally to the human heart than its opposite" (p. 622).

3. Martin Luther King, civil rights activist.

Martin Luther King admitted the profound influence of his parents. From his father, he learned a strong determination for justice, and from his mother, a gentle spirit. From both he gained a deep urge to serve humanity. The family's strong religious faith led him to the ministry.

King was awakened on December 1, 1955, when Rosa Parks was arrested in Montgomery, Alabama, for refusing to move to the back of the bus. After some doubt and much reflection, he decided to support the city bus boycott. He saw it as an act of civil disobedience, an act of noncooperation with an evil system. He was then elected president of the protest group. His fight for civil rights had begun. His models for action were Jesus and Gandhi, who refused to answer hatred with hatred, but only with love. He commented, "Nonviolent resistance had emerged as the technique of the movement, while love stood as the regulating ideal. In other words, Christ furnished the spirit and motivation while Gandhi furnished the method" (3).

King suffered greatly for his ideals. Within the ranks of his fellow activists, he was criticized for being nonviolent and seeking integration. He was arrested and jailed. He and his family were threatened with violence, and he was finally assassinated, like his hero, Gandhi. Yet, through all his hardships and the many peace marches, he maintained a hope expressed in his famous speech in Washington: "I have a dream that one day this nation will rise up and live out the true meaning of its creed—we hold these truths to be self-evident that all men are created equal. I have a dream that one day on the red hills of Georgia the sons of former slaves and the sons of former slave owners will be able to sit down together at the table of brotherhood" (p. 226).

4. Anne Frank, a girl with a resilient innocence.

Anne Frank, a young sensitive girl with wisdom beyond her years, wrote a diary (4) of her experience hiding from the Nazi Gestapo. She and her family lived in terror of being discovered and taken away to an extermination camp. Their crime? Being Jewish. Many of their family and friends were dragged away to suffer a terrible fate. They listened intently on their hidden radio for news of the progress of the war and heard war planes, bombs and guns firing outside their Amsterdam refuge. Anne wrote in her diary to her imaginary best friend, Kitty: "My nerves often get the better of me: it is especially on Sundays that I feel rotten. The atmosphere is so oppressive, and sleepy and as heavy as lead. You don't hear a single bird singing outside, and a deadly close silence hangs everywhere, catching hold of me as if it will drag me down deep into the underworld" (p. 113).

Despite her youthful innocence, she knew the horror and hatred of Hitler and the Gestapo. She saw herself and her family "surrounded by danger and darkness." Yet she did not hate those who sought to kill her and all the Jewish people. She did not despair. She did not lose courage. Anne continued to believe in humanity's essential goodness. She wrote: "It's really a wonder that I haven't dropped all my ideals, because they seem so absurd and impossible to carry out. Yet I keep them, because in spite of everything I still believe that people are really good at heart. I simply can't build up my hopes on a foundation consisting of confusion, misery, and death" (p. 263).

5. Mahatma Gandhi, a seeker of Truth.

From a young age, Mohandas Gandhi made a commitment to seek and live the Truth above all else. He said, "But one thing took deep root in me—the conviction that morality is the basis of things, and that truth is the substance of all morality. Truth became my sole objective....Return good for evil became my guiding principle" (5). Gandhi undertook personal experiments to discover what was true for him, in his religious practice, diet, studies, career, and social action.

When Gandhi moved to South Africa to work as an attorney, he had a conversion experience. While riding a train, the conductor told him to move because he was "colored." Gandhi refused. He was then thrown off the train and spent the night in silent reflection. He thought, "I began to think of my duty...The hardship to which I was subjected was superficial—only a symptom of the deep disease of colour prejudice. I should try, if possible, to root out the disease and suffer hardships in the process" (p. 97). He then took the next train to Pretoria and began his life's work to uproot discrimination in all its forms.

Gandhi remained faithful to his pursuit of truth at all costs, even to the point of death. His weapon in his work in both South Africa and India was "Satyagraha," which is dedication to truth. He believed people by nature were peaceful, not violent. Consequently, he pursued a path of nonviolence, non-cooperation, and peaceful resistance against unjust government practices. A vision of peace among all peoples and of an independent India based on religious pluralism sustained him. His dream was realized in South Africa with Nelson Mandela and in India where he was acknowledged as the "Father of the Nation." He affirmed the power of nonviolent love, saying, "In a gentle way you can shake the world."

The lives of these great figures reveal the qualities of authentic forgiveness. The following virtues occur naturally when you are simply yourself:

- Have patience and compassion for yourself and others.

- Give up the craving for comfort and pleasure.

- Maintain your innocence. Live your truth.

- Believe in the essential goodness of all.

- Are dedicated to the wellbeing of all, since all are connected.

- Commit to nonviolence.

- Let passion for justice inflame you.

Like these remarkable people, you must search your soul to discover who you are and what life demands of you. How are you, as an individual, to contribute? You have a unique calling, a gift that only you can give to the universe. Your life task is to discover that gift and share it. A story by the Persian poet Rumi expresses the uniqueness of your vocation:

"A King sent you to a country to carry out one special, specific task. You go to the country and you perform a hundred other tasks, but if you have not performed the task you were sent for, it is as if you have performed nothing at all. So man has come into the world for a particular task and that is his purpose. If he doesn't perform it, he will have done nothing" (6).

Your joy will come from discovering and living your life task.

Paradox of Giving and Receiving

In an angry state of mind, you live with a clenched fist. Preoccupied with having been harmed, you are in the self-protective mode. Feeling powerless, you are ready to fight. What are you fighting for? The list is endless: your sense of control, a loved one, your possessions, your good image, and so forth. You entertain the belief that if you hang on tightly enough you will be strong and secure. You also imagine that if you give up something, it is lost forever. Your threatened mind follows a zero-balance way of thinking. There is only a limited supply of whatever you desire, and once it is used up, it is gone.

The twelfth step of recovery insists on turning away from yourself to help others. The step confronts you with a paradox: "We give it away to keep it." That statement confounds the logic of your threatened mind. It challenges your self-centered urge to protect yourself at all costs. It invites you to open your hands to others. The paradox echoes the wisdom of the *Tao Te Ching*:

"Serve the needs of others,
And all your needs will be fulfilled.
Through selfless action, fulfillment is attained" (7).

How is that possible? Look around you with your enlarged consciousness. The earth continually gives without asking in return. It only invites you to participate in its ongoing cycle of renewal. The air you breathe, the food you eat, the water you drink, and the sunshine that warms you come from the abundance of the earth. That abundance comes from a hidden, eternal Source we may call God, Ultimate Reality, or the Life Force.

Gratitude for what you receive inspires your generosity. You give because you recognize you have already received so much more. Furthermore, you realize you are intimately connected with all. You love others as another self. In caring for them, you care for yourself. Often, by the law of attraction, the person who receives your love responds with love. It creates a bond of intimacy. Even if you do not receive appreciation or gratitude, you know in your heart you were true to yourself. In being yourself, you experience great joy and freedom.

Practice: Tonglen

A traditional Eastern practice to cultivate empathy and compassion is "Tonglen," which means "sending and receiving" (7). It counters your natural instinct to flee what is uncomfortable and chase after pleasure. Through this exercise, you receive with openness and compassion your own and others' suffering. Then you send out love and peace. The Dalai Lama related that he uses this practice to deepen his compassion for the Chinese. Here are the steps in the practice:

1) Sit comfortably in a quiet place with your eyes closed. Focus on the rising and falling of your breath. Breathe slowly and deeply, sensing peace and relaxation filling your body. With each breath, feel a sense of openness and spaciousness within your heart.

2) Next, still focusing on your breath, imagine that you are breathing in hot, black, dirty smoke that repulses you. Feel your repugnance as you breathe in the burning blackness. As you breathe out, imagine you are exhaling a cool, gentle, fresh breeze that fills the room. Imagine the bright freshness of the great outdoors coming from within you. Breathe in tarry smoke and breathe out fresh air.

3) Now, visualize yourself in pain because of your anger and the shame and guilt you feel for harming others. Do not avoid feeling the intensity of your suffering, as you usually do. Consciously embrace the pain. With each in-breath, feel that suffering as if it were hot, thick, black smoke. Breathe it in deeply, but do not hold on to it. With each natural out-breath, imagine exhaling peace and tranquility, as if it were cool, fresh air.

4) After several minutes of focusing on transforming your own suffering, visualize a person whom you harmed. Allow yourself to feel deeply the pain you caused them and your own remorse. Breathe in their suffering like black smoke, then, exhale a cooling peace. Sense your compassion as you breathe in their suffering and your love as you breathe out peace and joy.

5) Finally, imagine all the living creatures of the world and their suffering. Like you, all want to avoid sorrow and find happiness. Sense your oneness with the whole world. Inhale the suffering of the world and exhale happiness and peace.

You can use this exercise at any time, for even a few moments, with anyone you choose. It keeps you present to their suffering and helps develop empathy. The practice helps you nurture a compassionate, fearless heart, confident that the pain you encounter can never destroy you. In fact, the suffering, if embraced, can lead to new life.

The first eleven steps culminate in the twelfth step, a call to action. Your spiritual awakening loosened the bond to your hostile reactions, freeing you to pursue what you value most in life. Living your unique life task and serving others are the keys to finding joy and fulfillment.

Epilogue:
Flow of Forgiveness

> *"The weak can never forgive.*
> *Forgiveness is the attribute of the strong."*
>
> —Mahatma Gandhi

> *"To change yourself is not your mission.*
> *To change yourself is not your duty.*
> *To awaken to your true nature is your opportunity."*
>
> —Mooji

Jason's Story Continued

Resentment about losing his job consumed Jason. Going to work each day was only a painful reminder of how he had been wronged. He saw himself as a victim. He wanted to tell his boss off, but he knew he needed the job, so he stuffed his rage. At work, he just went through the motions. At home, his mood was sullen. He complained to his wife, but she became exhausted by his self-pity. Jason began to find some comfort in drinking. "At least then I can forget my troubles," he told himself.

His wife was concerned and frequently said, "Jason, you have to get some help."

But Jason resisted, saying, "I can handle this on my own." Secretly, though, he felt powerless to overcome his rage. He felt ashamed that he could not solve his own emotional problem. "Seeing a psychiatrist or therapist is only for crazy people," he told himself.

Then one day, Mark, a close friend whom he admired, had lunch with him. His friend was an alcoholic who had been sober for ten years. Jason had witnessed how he put the wreckage of his life back together after his uncontrolled drinking. He had lost his job and marriage. Now he was remarried and had a successful career. Mark said, "I'm concerned about you, Jason. I can see how miserable you are after losing that promotion. I'm also concerned about your drinking."

"I'm no alcoholic," Jason responded defensively.

"I'm not saying you are. There's a group that's meeting at the church where I attend AA meetings. Would you come with me? I think it could help you," Mark said.

Because Jason saw how Mark had overcome his problems and grown over the years, he responded, "I'll think about it."

A month later, Mark invited Jason to accompany him to the meeting at his church, and Jason agreed. Together, they entered a room with a sign, "Emotions Anonymous." A small group was gathered. Several members introduced themselves and welcomed the two of them warmly. Jason was impressed with their friendliness. The leader invited Jason and Mark to sit at a first step table. After a brief introduction, the first step was read, "We admitted we were powerless over our emotions and that our lives had become unmanageable." Each of the group members around the table reflected on the step and told their story of emotional struggle and freedom. Jason was impressed by their honesty and told himself, "Holy smokes! These people think like me and they're getting over it. It gives me hope" (1).

Good company is an indispensable aid on your journey towards freedom from your bondage to anger. When I was making my life-changing decision to leave the priesthood, I sought the help of a therapist and my priest fraternity. The weight of my conflicted emotions was too great to bear alone. In the same way, your struggle with anger may be lightened with the help of others.

Flow of Forgiveness

As this book has hopefully shown, the remedy for anger is forgiveness. That may seem an impossible medicine when you are addicted to rage. For example, Marilyn, a woman abused as a child by her parents and filled with self-hatred, told me she was stunned by a phrase she read in a book by Mitch Albom entitled *Tuesdays with Morrie*. Mitch's mentor, Morrie, encouraged Mitch, "Forgive everyone everything now." Marilyn protested, "That's impossible! How can I forgive my parents for all the terrible things they did to me? How can I ever stop blaming myself for being the horrible person I am?"

I assured her, "You can. It just takes time, effort, and prayer. You simply have to allow yourself to be yourself. That means dropping the anger and being your compassionate self. It is giving a gift to yourself and others, even if you think no one deserves it."

Coming to forgiveness is a process that involves several steps that follow the Twelve Steps:

- Step one: Embrace your anger.
- Steps two and three: Receive the gift of forgiveness.
- Steps four through seven: Forgive yourself.
- Steps eight and nine: Give and ask for the gift of forgiveness.

Fire in the Hole

You were born with a blazing fire in your psyche. It may be so frightening that you want to extinguish it so your ship does not sink. That fire is anger, an energy that gives both light and heat. It is a force for good or evil. It is something so powerful that it may seem stolen from the Gods. The Greek myth of Prometheus tells the story of a man who dared to steal fire from the Gods. In punishment, he was chained to a rock where an eagle ate his liver daily, the seat of emotions. Anger is a dangerous, immensely powerful gift that needs to be used wisely and well, or it can hold you in bondage.

The figures of the Dalai Lama, Martin Luther King, Nelson Mandela, Anne Frank, and Mahatma Gandhi exemplify persons who used their anger to the benefit of all. They had a burning desire for justice and became freedom fighters. They refused to hate their oppressors. Instead, they loved them but hated the unjust system, and the violent behavior the system provoked. They were strong individuals and models of forgiveness. Their tough love, while resisting any urges to be violent, changed society. They firmly believed that only love could overcome hatred.

In a similar way, your anger has the white fire of awareness. When provoked and understood, it possesses critical judgment that cuts through nonsense and illusions. It has the wisdom of clarity. You can use your anger to stand up for yourself, establish clear boundaries, and protest injustice to yourself and others. It gives you courage to live your truth. However, if your natural anger is suppressed out of fear or allowed to be indulged without wise restraint, it can be destructive to yourself and others. If you use your anger to control or manipulate others for your own selfish purposes, it will consume you.

The first step towards recovery from your anger addiction is to embrace and learn from your anger. You acknowledge your powerlessness over it and how your misuse of it has made your life unmanageable.

A Gift Received

Marilyn was right. If you have been wounded deeply enough, you cannot push yourself to forgive others. Steps one, two, and three affirm that, on your own, you are powerless over your anger. But turning to your Higher Power, you can find the strength to give up your anger and become compassionate toward those who harmed you. You experience the power of love, of being loved in your unworthiness. That frees you to love and forgive others. You do not need to be perfect. That is impossible, anyway. You do not have to work hard to prove your value. Besides, you cannot earn self-worth. You do not have to erase your past harmful deeds. The past is done. You can only open your heart to receive the gift of forgiveness from your Higher Power. Paul Tillich, the well-known theologian, defined grace: "Accept the fact that you are accepted, despite the fact that you are unacceptable."

Accepting the gift of forgiveness is no small task. Ask Judas. He preferred to hang himself rather than ask Jesus for forgiveness. He imagined his sin greater than God's mercy. To accept the gift of forgiveness is to give up control, because you can do nothing to earn it. You also cannot manipulate God to make it happen. You can only pray and wait with trust. A Gallup poll taken in 1991 indicated that 83% of more than 900 respondents claimed they needed God's help to forgive (2).

Furthermore, believing in forgiveness is difficult because you may see God as a harsh Judge, or the universe as hostile. There is no room for mercy. You may imagine that your God is as critical and vengeful as you are. However, all the world religions preach a loving God. Two-thirds of Jesus' teachings are directly or indirectly related to forgiveness. Nevertheless, your ability to forgive others will depend on your experience of being forgiven by God. In fact, you may experience God's forgiveness most powerfully through the mercy of others. Forgiveness is a free gift, never earned or deserved. Gratitude for the gift you received overflows in generosity to share that gift.

Forgive Yourself

Working steps four through seven, you realize the character defects that underlie your anger. The discovery of the magnitude of your self-centeredness may be overwhelming. The anger is only the tip of an iceberg of selfish desires. When you look in the mirror, you see that the enemy you most despise is yourself. That is why so much of your anger is directed against yourself. You may ask yourself how you can ever overcome all your faults. The answer—you cannot. You can make some progress, but you cannot reach perfection. In fact, you cannot even earn forgiveness for yourself.

Robert, a sincere Catholic who was wracked with guilt, told me, "I go to confession once a month because I know I'm so sinful. I believe God forgives me when the priest gives me absolution, but I don't know how to forgive myself. I'm 70 years old. There's no time for me to make up for all the terrible things I've done in my life."

"What makes you think you have to undo the past before you can be forgiven?" I asked. Robert kept his own personal accounting system.

"It's just that I feel so much shame and guilt. I don't know how to get rid of it," he responded.

I suggested that he did not have to get rid of those uncomfortable feelings. He only had to change his relationship to them. Instead of hating them, he could learn to love them and learn from them. "The Guest House," a poem by Rumi, expresses the power of acceptance (3):

This being human is a guest house.
Every morning a new arrival.
A joy, a depression, a meanness,
Some momentary awareness comes
As an unexpected visitor.

Welcome and entertain them all!
Even if they're a crowd of sorrows,
Who violently sweep your house
Empty of its furniture.

Still, treat each guest honorably.
He may be clearing you out
For some new delight.

The dark thought, the shame, the malice.
Meet them at the door laughing,
And invite them in.

Be grateful for whoever comes,
Because each has been sent
As a guide from beyond.

Giving and Asking for Forgiveness

Loving yourself wisely, you are freed to love others with a forgiving heart. In steps eight and nine, you reach out to others. Feeling loved by both God and yourself, you sense you are lovable. Then, you can see the goodness in others, who are human like you. You can look beyond the hurtful behavior, without minimizing its effect on you, and see the essential goodness of the offender. You can hate what the person did, but still love the person. With the wisdom and compassion gained in facing your own unworthiness, you become more accepting of the others' failings.

As much as you may want to forgive the offender, you may still feel stuck. For example, Suzanne, whose husband had an affair, said, "It's been ten years, and I still can't forgive my husband. I still hold a grudge. He has done everything he could to make up for it, but somehow it's not enough."

"Perhaps his betrayal touched on a deeper reservoir of pain, suggesting there is still some more unfinished business of healing," I suggested.

Suzanne nodded in agreement and said, "I've been betrayed many times in my life, going all the way back to my parents."

You hang on to your anger because you need it to defend yourself, often from deeper wounds. You displace the anger from people who harmed you in the past onto current relationships. Your efforts to forgive those who harmed you will cause a chain reaction of healing love back to your childhood. As you gradually let go of the hurt and anger, your wounds heal. An AA saying states, "Forgiveness of others is a gift to yourself."

The circle of love is complete when you acknowledge sincerely how you harmed others and ask for their forgiveness. Asking forgiveness requires humility and courage. You have no control over their response. Exposing your vulnerability, you risk rejection, but the gamble can pay unexpected dividends. Hatred's chain is smashed. Your guilt is relieved. The other's pain is acknowledged. A broken relationship is mended.

Forgiveness flows. Its source is your Higher Power. The love flows through you, inviting you to forgive yourself. You then allow the flow to embrace those who harmed you. Asking forgiveness of those you harmed invites them into the flow of love. Your motto for life becomes, to paraphrase the AA saying, "Just accept. Don't expect, judge, or reject."

Paradox of Time: Already and Not Yet

Jack, a man whose girlfriend cheated on him, asked, "How long will it take for me to get over this? I keep thinking about my girlfriend, and I get upset when any of my friends see her. I know you see other people who have gone through the same thing. How long did it take for them?"

"Everyone is different. It will take as long as you need. You hang on to your anger because it serves a purpose. You'll let it go when you are ready," I responded. I could have responded, "Forever or a day." Jack wanted a timetable, to know what to expect, which is a way of being in control. I recall the experience of Bill Wilson, the cofounder of Alcoholics Anonymous. He struggled for decades to become sober, on and off the wagon, in and out of hospitals. Then, he suddenly had a "flash conversion" and never took another drink. He became sober in an instant, but it took years for him to be ready.

Working the steps confronts you with another paradox of recovery: "You are already perfect, but still need to work on it." Addicted to anger, you lost your true self. Your hostile habitual reactions are not who you really are. Your automatic reacting protects you from imagined threats. However, it veils your true identity. A false, defensive self has taken over. You work the steps to uncover your true self, which is naturally kind and compassionate. When you awaken to the truth of who you really are, you are free. What you fail to recognize is that you are already free, but have chosen bondage to anger without fully realizing it.

Recovery is like discovering a treasure, which is already in plain sight, but that you are blind to. A traditional story told by Sri Ramana Maharishi, an Indian sage, illustrates this truth: "A lady had a precious necklace around her neck. Once, in her excitement, she forgot it and thought she lost the necklace. She became anxious and looked for it in her home but could not find it. She asked her friends and neighbors if they knew anything about the necklace. They did not. At last a kind friend of hers told her to feel the necklace round her neck. She found that it had all along been round her neck and she was happy. When others asked her later if she had found the necklace which was lost, she said, 'Yes, I have found it.' She still felt she had recovered a lost jewel" (4).

You began working the steps because you felt imperfect. Your anger disturbed you. Your life had become unmanageable. As you worked the steps, it dawned on you that you had lost yourself in your anger. You discovered that what you believed threatened you could not really harm you at the core of who you are. You were fighting a ghost, captivated by an illusion. Through recovery, you recognized your true self that was there all along. Mooji, the sage from Jamaica, taught, "It often takes a long time to recognize the gift already in your hands" (5).

You are born free, free to be yourself. You only have to claim your birthright.

Endnotes

Introduction

1. Robert Enright and Richard Fitzgibbons, *Forgiveness Therapy* (Washington, DC: American Psychological Association, 2015).

2. Dennis Ortman, *Anxiety Anonymous: The Big Book on Anxiety Addiction* (Hollister, CA: MSI Press, 2015) and Dennis Ortman, *Depression Anonymous: The Big Book on Depression Addiction* (Hollister: MSI Press, 2016).

3. All quotes from the *Tao Te Ching* are from Stephen Mitchell's translation, *Tao Te Ching*(New York: Harper Perennial Classics, 2000).

Chapter Three

1. Daniel Goleman, *Emotional Intelligence* (New York: Bantam Books, 1995), 3-29.

Chapter Four

1. All the Steps/Traditions quotes are from *Twelve Steps and Twelve Traditions* (New York: Alcoholics Anonymous World Services, Inc., 2012), 40.

2. All the Big Book quotes are from *Alcoholics Anonymous: The Big Book*, fourth edition (New York: Alcoholics Anonymous World Services, Inc., 2001), 62.

Chapter Five

1. *Alcoholics Anonymous,* 1-16.

2. Charles Duhigg, *The Power of Habit* (New York: Random House, 2012), 84-85.

3. All the Emotions Anonymous quotes are from *Emotions Anonymous*, revised edition (Saint Paul: Emotions Anonymous International Services, 1994).

Chapter Six

1. *Emotions Anonymous*, 13.

2. Jon Kabat-Zinn, *Full Catastrophe Living* (New York: Bantam Books, 2013), 54-74.

Chapter Seven

1. Diana Butler Bass, *Christianity After Religion: The End of Church and the Birth of a New Spiritual Awakening* (New York: HarperOne, 2012), 46.

2. The 2008 Pew Study as reported in Bass, 49.

3. Reported in Bass, 49.

4. *Alcoholics Anonymous*, 12.

5. Recounted in Christina Grof, *The Thirst for Wholeness* (New York: HarperCollins, 1993), 33-34.

6. All quotes are from Gregory Hays' translation of Marcus Aurelius, *Meditations* (New York: Random House Modern Library, 2002), 7:59.

7. All quotes from Mooji, *White Fire* (United Kingdom: Mooji Media Publications, 2014), 144.

8. Joseph Goldstein, *Insight Meditation* (Boston: Shambhala, 2003).

Chapter Eight

1. Thich Nhat Hanh, *Anger* (New York: Riverhead Books, 2001).

2. Sharon Salzburg, *Loving-Kindness* (Boston: Shambhala, 2002).

Chapter Nine

1. Nisargadatta Maharaj, *I Am That.* (Durham: Acorn Press, 1973), 246.

2. Thomas Keating, *Divine Therapy and Addiction* (New York: Lantern Books, 2009), 47-55.

3. Romans 7:15, 22. All Bible quotes are from *The New American Bible* (New Jersey: Thomas Nelson, 1971).

4. Shantideva, *The Way of the Bodhisattva*, trans. Padmakara Translation Group (Boston: Shambhala, 1997), verse 48.

Chapter Ten

1. Story related in Sharon Salzburg and Robert Thurman, *Love Your Enemy* (New York: Hay House, 2013), 66.

2. Thomas Keating, *The Heart of the World* (New York: Crossroad Publishing, 2008), 47-55.

Chapter Eleven

1. Quoted in Richard Rohr, *Breathing Under Water* (Cincinnati: St. Anthony Messenger Press, 2011), 103.

2. Gregg Krech, *Naikan: Gratitude, Grace, and the Japanese Art of Self-Reflection* (Berkeley: Stone Bridge Press, 2002).

Chapter Twelve

1. Thomas Merton, *New Seeds of Contemplation* (New York: New Directions Publ., 1972), 36.

2. Dalai Lama, *Art of Happiness* (New York: Riverhead Books, 1998), 68.

3. Keating, Thomas, *Open Mind, Open Heart* (New York: Bloomsbury, 2006).

Chapter Thirteen

1. Dalai Lama, *Wisdom of Forgiveness* (New York: Riverhead Books, 2004), 47.

2. Nelson Mandela, *Long Walk to Freedom* (New York: Little, Brown, and Company, 2013), 624.

3. Martin Luther King, *The Autobiography of Martin Luther King, Jr.* (New York: Grand Central, 1998), 67.

4. Anne Frank, *The Diary of a Young Girl* (New York: Bantam Books, 1993).

5. Mohandas K. Gandhi, *Autobiography* (New York: Dover Publications, 1983), 30.

6. Story told in Llewellyn Vaughan-Lee, *Love is a Fire* (Pointe Reyes Station: The Golden Sufi Center, 2013), 45-46.

7. Pema, Chodron, *The Places that Scare You* (Boston: Shambhala, 2001), 55-60.

Epilogue

1. You can find the Emotions Anonymous website on the Internet to find meetings in your area.

2. Reported in Enright, p. 149.

3. Coleman Barks, *The Essential Rumi* (London: Penguin, 2004), 109.

4. Ramana Maharishi, Ed. David Godman, *Be As You Are: The Teachings of Sri Ramana Maharishi* (London: Arkana, 1985), pp. 31-32.

5. Mooji, 620.

Dennis Ortman, Ph.D.

Suggested Readings

On Anger

Beck, Aaron. *Prisoner's of Hate: The Cognitive Basis of Anger, Hostility, and Violence*. New York: HarperCollins, 1999.

This book by one the founders of cognitive-behavioral therapy explains how distorted thinking leads to angry emotions and aggressive behavior.

Brandt, Andrea. *Mindful Anger: A Pathway to Emotional Freedom*. New York: W.W. Norton, 2014.

Using the tool of mindfulness, Brandt shows ways of transforming the destructive energy of anger into a positive force to achieve your life goals.

Engel, Beverly. *Honor Your Anger: How Transforming Your Anger Style Can Change Your Life*. Hoboken: John Wiley and Sons, 2004.

In this book, Engel recommends avoiding the extremes of suppressing or indulging your anger. Becoming acquainted with your personal anger style, she suggests ways of using the energy of your anger beneficially.

Lerner, Harriet. *The Dance of Anger: A Woman's Guide to Changing the Patterns of Intimate Relationships*. New York: Perennial Library, 1989.

In this classic book, Lerner addresses women's struggles with anger. She shows how women can turn their anger into a constructive force for reshaping their lives and renewing their relationships.

Dennis Ortman, Ph.D.

On the Twelve Steps

Twelve Steps and Twelve Traditions. New York: Alcoholics Anonymous World Services, 2012.

Written by the cofounder of Alcoholics Anonymous, this classic text explains how the Steps are a powerful tool for recovery. The book explains in detail the rationale of each step and how to implement them for recovery.

Shapiro, Rami. *Recovery—the Sacred Art: The Twelve Steps as Spiritual Practice.* Woodstock: SkyLight Paths Publishing, 2013.

Shapiro explains the spiritual approach of the Twelve Steps from the universal perspective of world religions. He offers many practices to deepen the impact of the Steps.

Keating, Thomas. *Divine Therapy and Addiction: Centering Prayer and the Twelve Steps.* New York: Lantern Books, 2009.

In the form of an interview, Keating, a Cistercian monk, elaborates the wisdom of the Twelve Steps from a Christian perspective.

On Forgiveness

Enright, Robert. *Forgiveness is a Choice: A Step-by-Step Process for Resolving Anger and Restoring Hope.* Washington, DC: American Psychological Association, 2001.

Based on his research as a psychologist, Enright presents a step-by-step process for resolving anger and developing peace through the exercise of authentic forgiveness.

Salzburg, Sharon, and Thurman, Robert. *Love Your Enemy.* New York: Hay House, 2013.

Written from a Buddhist perspective, this book demonstrates a path for confronting the inner and outer enemy of anger and developing compassion, patience, and love in the process.

Singer, Michael. *The Untethered Soul: The Journey Beyond Yourself.* Oakland: New Harbinger, 2007.

Drawing from both eastern and western wisdom traditions, Singer leads you on a journey to freedom from anger and other destructive emotions and thinking.

Select MSI Books

Self-Help Books

A Woman's Guide to Self-Nurturing (Romer)

Anxiety Anonymous: The Big Book on Anxiety Addiction (Ortman)

Creative Aging: A Baby Boomer's Guide to Successful Living (Vassiliadis & Romer)

Divorced! Survival Techniques for Singles over Forty (Romer)

Living Well with Chronic Illness (Charnas)

Publishing for Smarties: Finding a Publisher (Ham)

Survival of the Caregiver (Snyder)

The Marriage Whisperer: How to Improve Your Relationship Overnight (Pickett)

The Rose and the Sword: How to Balance Your Feminine and Masculine Energies (Bach & Hucknall)

The Widower's Guide to a New Life (Romer)

Widow: A Survival Guide for the First Year (Romer)

Inspirational and Religious Books

A Believer-Waiting's First Encounters with God (Mahlou)

A Guide to Bliss: Transforming Your Life through Mind Expansion (Tubali)

El Poder de lo Transpersonal (Ustman)

Everybody's Little Book of Everyday Prayers (MacGregor)

Joshuanism (Tosto)

Puertas a la Eternidad (Ustman)

The Gospel of Damascus (O. Imady)

The Seven Wisdoms of Life: A Journey into the Chakras (Tubali)

When You're Shoved from the Right, Look to Your Left: Metaphors of Islamic Humanism (O. Imady)

Memoirs

Blest Atheist (Mahlou)

Forget the Goal, the Journey Counts . . . 71 Jobs Later (Stites)

Healing from Incest: Intimate Conversations with My Therapist (Henderson & Emerton)

It Only Hurts When I Can't Run: One Girl's Story (Parker)

Las Historias de Mi Vida (Ustman)

Losing My Voice and Finding Another (C. Thompson)

Of God, Rattlesnakes, and Okra (Easterling)

Road to Damascus (E. Imady)

Still Life (Mellon)

Foreign Culture

Syrian Folktales (M. Imady)

The Rise and Fall of Muslim Civil Society (O. Imady)

The Subversive Utopia: Louis Kahn and the Question of National Jewish Style in Jerusalem (Sakr)

Thoughts without a Title (Henderson)

Popular Psychology

Road Map to Power (Husain & Husain)

The Seeker (Quinelle)

Understanding the People around You: An Introduction to Socionics (Filatova)

Humor

Mommy Poisoned Our House Guest (C. B. Leaver)

The Musings of a Carolina Yankee (Amidon)

Parenting

365 Teacher Secrets for Parents: Fun Ways to Help Your Child in Elementary School (McKinley & Trombly)

How to Be a Good Mommy When You're Sick (Graves)

Lessons of Labor (Aziz)

CPSIA information can be obtained
at www.ICGtesting.com
Printed in the USA
LVHW020132210723
752888LV00006B/61